Luna Blanca's Tarot Book

Luna Blanca's Tarot Book

———————

With Illustrations From
The Tranquil Willows Deck

A *ByTheLightOf* Publication

©2015 ByTheLightOf

All rights reserved.

No part of this book may be reproduced
in any manner whatsoever without written
permission except in the case of brief
quotations embodied in critical essays
and articles.

Cover Image: The World from the Tranquil
Willows Tarot Deck by Tranquillity Fearn
and Rowen Saille rowensaille@gmail.com.
Used with permission.

Cover Design by Christian DeLaO

Interior Design by Shawn Aveningo, The Poetry Box®

Interior Images from the Tranquil Willows
Tarot Deck by Tranquillity Fearn and
Rowen Saille rowensaille@gmail.com
Used with permission.

Diagrams by Christian DeLaO

Library of Congress Control Number: 2015953192

ISBN-13: 978-0-6925314-9-5
ISBN-10: 069253149-1

Printed in the United States of America.

ByTheLightOf Publication
www.ByTheLightOf.com

Contents

Preface vii

About the Tarot 1

The Cards

Major Arcana

    The Fool 8
    The Magician 11
    The High Priestess 15
    The Empress 19
    The Emperor 23
    The Hierophant 27
    The Lovers 31
    The Chariot 35
    Justice 39
    The Hermit 43
    The Wheel 47
    Strength 50
    The Hanged One 53
    Death 56
    Temperance 59
    The Devil 63
    The Tower 67
    The Star 71
    The Moon 74
    The Sun 78
    Judgement 81
    The World 84

Minor Arcana

    The Suits 88
        Aces 89
        Twos 94
        Threes 99
        Fours 104
        Fives 109
        Sixes 114
        Sevens 119
        Eights 124
        Nines 129
        Tens 134
    The Court Cards 139
        Pages 140
        Knights 145
        Queens 150
        Kings 155

Reading the Cards
    Getting Started 162
    Advanced Readings 169
    Reading for Others 186

Numerology and Tarot 190

Tarot for Meditation and Spiritual Intent 198

About the Author 205

About the Artists 207

Works Cited 209

Suggested Reading 211

Preface

I began working with Tarot over 20 years ago. The first deck of cards I learned was the round, Goddess-centered Motherpeace Deck. I began by teaching myself the cards via daily practice and by studying Vicki Noble's book *Motherpeace: A Way to the Goddess through Myth, Art, and Tarot*. Within three years, I started reading for friends. Within six years, I began reading and teaching the cards professionally, both face-to-face and online.

Two of my students from that period, Rowen Saille and Tranquillity Fearn, felt frustrated with trying to read the card orientations on a round deck. "Was the card more upright or titled back?" they asked. "And what happens when the cards spin further after laying them out?" This experience with round cards inspired them to create their own deck, a triangular deck, which makes card orientations easier to read. This deck became the beautiful Tranquil Willows Tarot which illustrates this book.

It is important to note, however, that this book is not written to provide interpretations specific to Tranquil Willows. Instead this book reflects my experience as a multi-deck Tarot reader and teacher over the past few decades. To this end, I've used traditional card names. For example I use the traditional name *knights* instead of the Tranquil Willows designation *warriors*.

When I assign gender to a card, I am reflecting the gender given that character in a traditional deck, not in the Tranquil Willows deck. Be aware, however, that this gender is not literal. It could represent a man or a woman. In fact, you will read sentences like this: "She is an earth mother, the ultimate nurturer (even if she is a man)." This is not commenting in any way on a person's sexuality or the gender he or she identifies with. This is simply a necessary and expedient way to talk about an archetype.

My interpretation of the cards has been formed by working first with the Motherpeace deck, then with Aleister Crowley's Thoth deck, and later with many other decks. This type of comparative Tarot is a branch of study based on what I call *the whole orange theory*. Think of each Tarot Card as an orange. Any one deck will only present one section of that orange. The more decks studied, the more sections will appear. Not all sections will apply at once. Some may never apply. However the more we work with the Tarot, the closer we will come to knowing *the whole orange* for each card.

In this book, I have included a comparison of the images in several decks to reveal a range of interpretations for each card. The decks I discuss most are Motherpeace; Crowley's Thoth; Kris Waldherr's two decks, Goddess Tarot and Lover's Path; Robin Wood's deck; New Vision; Rider-Waite-Smith; and of course Tranquil Willows. See *About the Tarot* for more information about these decks.

For each Major Arcana card, I have included keywords; a general interpretation; *Dark Side* which may apply to reversed cards; *Light Side* which suggests an activity; *Between the Decks* which is described above; *In Spiritual Work* which suggests ways to use the card in meditation, prayer, or ritual; *Questions to Ask* for reflecting on the application of the card; *Affirmations* for integrating the message of the card; and *Snapshot* which provides a haikuesque poem encapsulating the feeling of the card.

For each Minor Arcana card, I have included a multi-deck comparison and a general interpretation. Keywords are provided for each number and face card, for example, keywords for the Aces, the Twos, and so forth. A brief discussion of the suits and the court cards is also included. In both the Major and Minor Arcana, I have presented some commentary on how the cards work in combination with each other.

In addition to card interpretations, this book includes instructional chapters. *Reading the Cards* begins with one-card spreads and builds up to complex spreads. It also includes advice on reading for others and on learning multiple decks. *Numerology and Tarot* gives instructions for calculating a person's Name, Lifetime, and Year Symbols, and an explanation of how those symbols interact. The *Major Arcana* chapter includes additional sections for the nine Tarot cards that correspond to the nine-year numerology cycle. For example, *The Magician as Lifetime Symbol* can be found with other explanations of the Magician card. The last chapter, *Tarot for Meditation and Spiritual Intent*, shows how to explore Tarot cards in meditation and incorporate the cards in prayer and ritual.

Thus, this book is intended as both a reference work and a textbook. If you have never worked with the cards before, this book is a good starting place. If you are already familiar with the cards and seek to deepen your knowledge, this book should be helpful. Some of the information in this book has appeared in my White Moon Studies course, on my *By The Light Of* website or Facebook page, and in my workshops.

I hope you enjoy your journey with the cards as much as I continue to enjoy mine.

Luna Blanca
2015

Luna Blanca's Tarot Book

About The Tarot

The 78-card Tarot deck originated in the early to mid 1400s in Italy. The 56-card *Minor Arcana* is based on early playing cards, being divided into four suits. The Tarot adds 22 Trumps or *Major Arcana*. Only 17 cards have survived from the oldest Tarot deck currently in existence, the Gringonneur deck. However the Tarot of Marseilles, created around 1500, is complete and available to modern readers who will clearly recognize the Trump images. The Sola Busca deck, contemporary with the Tarot of Marseilles, is the only ancient deck to illustrate the Minor Arcana with characters instead of the symbols used on playing cards. This deck has been reproduced in a limited edition under the name the Ancient Enlightened Tarot.

Many scholars believe the cards were perpetuated in the West to safeguard certain teachings through the Dark Ages and the Inquisition. While scholars do not agree on what those secret teachings might have been, the cards do seem to be coded in some way: Tarot images tend to evoke strong emotional responses, pulling the viewer into the realm of folklore, mythology, and legend. As Richard Cavendish notes in *The Tarot*, "They give the impression of holding the key to some vital secret which cannot quite be put into words, which is almost in the mind's grasp when it slips elusively away."

This lure of hidden knowledge attracted Eliphas Levi to the Tarot in the mid 1800s. During this time, America and England were undergoing a fascination with mysticism which supported a growing interest in the Tarot. Informed by a professional Paris-based fortuneteller named Alliette, Levi wrote a treatise on the cards that proved to be highly influential. One important group he influenced was the Order of the Golden Dawn which was formed in the 1880s. Although short-lived, this Order highlighted the Tarot in its teachings, and members of this group were key in shaping the Tarot as we know it today.

Golden Dawn member Arthur Edward Waite, together with artist Pamela Coleman Smith, created the Tarot deck that later came to be viewed as the standard deck and that remains the best-known deck today. Although she did not receive credit for her work during her lifetime, Smith changed the standard of the Minor Arcana from geometric symbols to detailed scenes illustrating human actions. Her images were inspired by those on the Sola Busca deck. Waite changed the name and the order of some Major Arcana cards to fit his spiritual philosophy.

Aleister Crowley, another member of the Golden Dawn, also created his own deck which is still popular today. He named his deck after the Egyptian god Thoth, and like Waite changed the names of some of the Trump cards. Unlike Waite who looked to ancient decks for the main images on the cards, Crowely completely reinterpreted the images in collaboration with artist Lady Freida Harris. Their cards are rich in Cabalistic, astrological, and mythological symbols. However their Minor Arcana cards are less detailed than those in Waite's deck.

After the spiritualist craze of the 1800s died down, Tarot gained a new foothold through the revival of Paganism and through Jungian psychology. Neopaganism was popularized in America and England by Margaret Murray in the early 1900s and by Gerald Gardener, a colleague of Crowley's, in the mid 1900s. Tarot remains popular today among Murray's and Gardener's spiritual heirs. Another influential figure is Carl Jung, founder of analytical psychology. While his theories were not influenced by the Tarot, he did acknowledge the Tarot in his work. Jung notes in *Archetypes of the Collective Unconscious* that "the set of pictures in the Tarot cards were distantly descended from the archetypes of transformation." The popularity of Jung's theories has increased interest in the Tarot over the last century.

Traditionally, Tarot has been used for divination, seeing what is hidden, sometimes in the future, sometimes in the past or present. This is still a common usage for the cards. But the Tarot is just as likely to be used as an aid for psychological transformation, tapping into archetypes: "the symbol of the sun, or the symbol of the man hung up by the feet, or the tower struck by lightning, or the wheel of fortune" in Jung's words. The images on the cards are the most powerful aspect of the Tarot. Over a thousand decks, with a wide variety of images, are currently in print.

This book describes images from eight different decks. Two are discussed above. **Rider-Waite-Smith**, first published in 1909 by William Rider And Son of London, is referred to as the traditional deck because many decks that came later are based on the images, names, and numbering here, and because the images in this deck are consistent with the most ancient Tarot images. **Crowley's Thoth**, first published in 1944, evidences art deco influences in the design. Crowley's name is included in discussions of this deck to distinguish it from other decks with the Thoth title.

The other decks discussed in this book are more modern. The round Goddess-centered cards, **Motherpeace**, were created by Vicki Noble and Karen Vogel and first published in 1983. This was the first round deck produced. This deck presents a complete departure from tradition. Drawing on multi-cultural and multi-ethnic imagery, each card reflects a feminist message. As discussed in *Court Cards* later in this book, Motherpeace brought an entirely new perspective to Tarot's face cards, changing the names and gender-associations. Motherpeace had a strong influence on later decks.

Artist Kris Waldherr created two decks discussed in this book: **Goddess Tarot** published in 1999 and **Lover's Path** published in

2004. The artist's name is included to distinguish these decks from other decks with similar names and to highlight the differences between Waldherr's decks. In Goddess Tarot, Waldherr illustrates the Major Arcana with goddesses from cultures around the word. The Minor Arcana does not reflect a wide departure from traditional decks, but is illustrated with ethnic diversity. Lover's Path takes a unique approach. The Major Arcana is peopled with famous lovers from Western history, from Odysseus and Penelope to Romeo and Juliet. Each Minor Arcana suit is focused on the story of a different couple. For example, all the coins reflect the story of Danae and Zeus.

Artist **Robin Wood** published her Pagan-centered Tarot deck in 1998. While these cards are based on traditional images, her Major Arcana depicts Neopagan versions of those archetypes. For example, the Magician wears a deer hood with antlers and the High Priestess holds a crystal ball. Her Minor Arcana also reinterprets the images to some degree, as seen in the Seven of Wands where the defender is dressed in a battle kilt. Nicknamed "the naked people deck," Wood's illustrations include more full-frontal nudity than most other decks do.

Tarot of the New Vision, published by Llewellyn in 2003, shows a rear view of the images from traditional decks. This technique enabled the artists to reveal, for example, what acolytes are doing behind the Hierophant's back (handling a snake) and what Strength sees in the distance (a stone giant). This behind-the-scenes glimpse into each card allows readers to deepen their interpretations. This deck includes subtitles in Italian, Spanish, French, and German, with main titles in English, allowing for further study.

The Tranquil Willows Tarot was created in 2001 but remained unpublished until 2015. The images in this deck were inspired by Motherpeace, Robin Wood, and traditional images. However, artists Tranquillity Fearn and Rowen Saille brought their unique vision to the cards displayed and discussed throughout this book. This deck presents rectangular images on black triangular backgrounds. Other triangular decks have been produced, but they are not widely available. Visit ByTheLightOf.com for information about purchasing this deck.

The Cards:

Major Arcana

0 The Fool

New Possibilities and Exploration

The first of the Major Arcana, the Fool often appears in a reading when we are at a new beginning – or yearn for one – whether we consciously realize that or not. The Fool indicates that you are feeling open to more possibilities than you usually consider. This is a time when you may surprise yourself with your actions. The Fool encourages you to release some restraints on your impulse control, to be more playful than you usually are. As adults, we crave labels, a framework, and directions. But when young children play, they simply move from one experience to the next without any plan in mind. Similarly, the Fool doesn't need to know where he's headed. Being willing to follow such an ambling path often requires a leap of faith, which is why in traditional decks he is shown stepping off a cliff. But the Fool is not suicidal. He knows he will not fall.

Dark Side

The Fool sometimes appears when you are feeling foolish or are afraid others will think you are foolish. Taken to the extreme, such fear can make you rigid, dogmatic, even tyrannical at times. If you have been digging in your heels, try a new strategy: ask for what will help you to feel safe and respected.

Light Side

The Fool sometimes appears when we find ourselves being a bit more childish than we normally are. While *being childish* can be negative, it can also signal that we are in need of more play. This card encourages us to play like a child – gardening, finger-painting, baking, or engaging in some other hands-on craft.

Between the Decks

Both Motherpeace and Tranquil Willows pictured here emphasize the playful aspects of this card. Both show physical joy, a handstand and a balletic leap respectively. Both picture a stream, indicating the flow of life. In contrast, Crowley's Thoth and New Vision emphasize the dangerous aspects of this card. Crowley's Thoth shows the Fool being bitten by a tiger, and New Vision shows an erupting volcano up ahead. Yet in both decks, the Fool is not in real danger: the tiger bite is playful, and the volcano is far away. Waldherr names this card Innocence in Lover's Path and Beginnings in Goddess Tarot.

In Spiritual Work

The Fool can be used in spiritual work. Try exploring ways to make a new beginning through the meditation exercises in the last chapter of this book using the Fool card as a focus. This card can also be used to draw a new beginning into your life via prayer or ritual. Lay the Fool on your altar along with the Six that embodies the new beginning you desire: the Six of Discs for a fresh start with health, money-management, family, or friendship; the Six of Swords to relocate or move on; the Six of Wands to be promoted or gain a new job; or the Six of Cups for a fresh start in love or spiritual practice. See the *Tarot for Meditation and Spiritual Intent* chapter for further discussion.

Questions to Ask

What am I telling myself *no* about right now? What would happen if I said *yes*?

What pleasure have I been postponing? Is there a way to indulge this?

What is attracting my attention right now?

Affirmations

I am open to exploring new possibilities.

I allow myself to play.

I go towards what attracts, away from what doesn't.

Snapshot

The Fool

Bungee jump
free fall:
embrace the sky

1 The Magician

Envisioning and Manifesting

When the Magician appears in a reading, you are more likely to get what you ask for. Even seemingly impossible situations can be turned around with a magical solution. The ingredients you need to provide are awareness and audacity. We often miss unusual windows of opportunity because we're not looking for them. The Magician encourages you to look. We also miss too-good-to-be-true chances because we lack the boldness to grab them. The Magician encourages you to speak up and take action, even when your conservative nature is balking at the prospect. The Magician energy often provides a little bit of extra luck. Paying attention and seizing the moment are all that are required. When the Magician appears in a reading with the Hierophant or the Fool, you are being warned that the solution to your problem will be unconventional and perhaps even seemingly foolish. However, when you are willing to take risks, magic happens.

Dark Side

The Magician can make life miserable for others when he doesn't get his way. If you or someone else has been acting out personal dramas, take a step back and examine the situation carefully. Perhaps the Magician can be appeased in a way that makes others comfortable too, and everyone can be happier.

Light Side

What magical powers do you wish you had? Allowing yourself to daydream along those lines is not only fun but will give you useful information. For example, if you'd like to be able to clean the kitchen with a twitch of your nose, perhaps you can hire a cleaning service or delegate the task.

Between the Decks

Most decks emphasize alchemy in the Magician card, the transformation of one material into another. Tranquil Willows pictured here provides the most modern interpretation, showing the Magician working in a chemistry lab. The Lover's Path, Robin Wood, and the traditional Rider-Waite-Smith show one or more practitioners in front of a table or altar, working with the elements of earth, air, fire, and water. Crowley's Thoth and Waldherr's Goddess Tarot show a god or goddess at work ordering the universe: Thoth-Hermes-Mercury in Crowley's deck and Isis in Waldherr's. All emphasize that change can be effected through action and will.

As Lifetime Symbol or Name Symbol

A person with the Magician as Lifetime or Name Symbol is an initiator. He has an amazing ability to line up opportunities for himself and others and can turn ideas into reality with a simple wave of his wand – or so it appears to those around him. On the other side of the coin, the Magician may expect instant results and may expect things to go his way at all times; thus he can be impatient, even petulant, when things don't turn out as he had planned. Magicians tend to be passionate people, attracted to the element of fire, and may struggle to master their tempers. They tend to be excellent communicators. See the *Numerology* chapter for a discussion of symbols.

As Year Symbol

The Magician year nearly always brings a major transition in one or more areas of a person's life – relationships, work, family, home, or self. This is the beginning of a new nine-year cycle and often marks the beginning of a new path, as both fate and willpower conspire to bring about change. People in a Magician year may have to walk through a lot of confusion and not-knowing because they can't see where the year will take them. However, they have a magnified ability to attract new opportunities. A Magician year is an excellent time to ask for a raise, buy a home, or secure a contract. See the *Numerology* chapter for a discussion of symbols.

In Spiritual Work

The Magician can be used in spiritual work. Try clarifying what you want to manifest in your life through the meditation exercises in the last chapter of this book using the Magician card as a focus. This card can also be used to manifest what you want via prayer or ritual. Lay the Magician on your altar along with the Ace that embodies what you want to attract: the Ace of Discs for health, security, or money; the Ace of Swords for insight or honesty; the Ace of Wands for revitalization or a fast resolution; or the Ace of Cups for love, happiness, or spiritual connection. See the *Tarot for Meditation and Spiritual Intent* chapter for further discussion.

Questions to Ask

Am I clear about what I want? How can I maintain awareness of my intent today?

In what ways is my life magical? How can I invite more magic into my life?

Am I comfortable being bold when needed? What changes do I need to make in this area of my life?

Affirmations

I ask and it is given me; I seek and I find; I knock and the door is opened unto me.

I seize the day.

Snapshot

The Magician

In the wake of his stardust smile
every head turns
says *yes*

2 The High Priestess

Hidden Knowledge and Intuition

The High Priestess' message is *trust your intuition*. You already have all the answers you need even though you may not have consciously acknowledged them. Now is not the time to seek others' advice. Instead, focus on inner reflection. This could be as simple as solitary think-time over a cup of tea or as complex as formal spiritual study. Meditating, journaling, or talking over the issue with a trusted friend can also help, especially if you make time for this on a regular basis. During times of difficulty, this card reminds you to rely upon spiritual tools for comfort and strength. Sometimes drawing the High Priestess indicates that you can see the truth of a situation far more clearly than others can. When combined with the Five of Wands, Seven of Wands, or Three of Swords, use extra caution when sharing your insights – they may not be welcome.

Dark Side

Sometimes High Priestesses are required to undergo a long journey sustained only by inner resources. This may be a difficult period where a source of former nourishment has dried up. When that is the case, the High Priestess reminds you to find alternate ways to nourish and care for yourself.

Light Side

Sometimes drawing the High Priestess indicates that it's time to *clean house* based on newfound clarity. This can manifest in physical ways, such as sorting through your closets, or psychological ways, such as bowing out of commitments that are no longer right for you. Such activities will feel freeing.

Between the Decks

Named Wisdom in Waldherr's Goddess Tarot and Lover's Path, most decks emphasize esoteric knowledge. Tranquil Willows pictured here shows the seeker in direct contact with the mysteries of nature – darkness, fire, the moon – while other decks draw on more formal traditions. Robin Wood emphasizes Pagan practices, Motherpeace emphasizes African tribal ceremonies, and New Vision along with most traditional decks emphasizes Judeo-Christian symbology. Most decks show a skilled practitioner making contact with the spiritual world. Waldherr's Goddess Tarot depicts the Hindu goddess Sarasvati. Crowley's Thoth includes a small camel symbol, emphasizing the message in *Dark Side* above.

As Lifetime Symbol or Name Symbol

A person with the High Priestess as Lifetime or Name Symbol is a seer. Her intuition is her strength; she can glance at a murky situation and see the underlying truth with clarity. This can be a very desirable trait; her friends often come to her for help. But this ability has its downside too. She can worry too much about hidden thoughts and feelings that will never manifest as reality. High Priestesses make excellent teachers, transmitting their insights to others. They are strongly drawn to spiritual study, and if they ignore this urge, it will continue to nag at them until they fulfill it. See the *Numerology* chapter for a discussion of symbols.

As Year Symbol

The High Priestess year brings important insights. People in a High Priestess year are challenged to recognize ongoing patterns in their thinking and behavior, including patterns in the types of people and situations they draw into their lives. Such knowledge may be coupled with spiritual study or psychotherapy. People in a High Priestess year will have no peace until they are willing to undergo this task. If they attempt to avoid this self-examination, painful life situations will prod them in that direction. As they gain insights about themselves, others will be drawn to them. Since High Priestesses are also teachers, they may find some pupils knocking at their door. See the *Numerology* chapter for a discussion of symbols.

In Spiritual Work

The High Priestess can be used in spiritual work. Try accessing your inner-wisdom about a certain situation through the meditation exercises in the last chapter of this book using the High Priestess card as a focus. This card can also be used to draw new understanding into your life via prayer or ritual. Lay the High Priestess on your altar along with the Eight that embodies what you want to better understand: the Eight of Discs to better understand your personal-growth challenges; the Eight of Swords to better understand your limitations; the Eight of Wands to better understand the flow of energy in a situation; or the Eight of

Cups to better understand what you need to walk away from. See the *Tarot for Meditation and Spiritual Intent* chapter for further discussion.

Questions to Ask

In what situations am I frustrated by other people's inability to see clearly?

Is it better for me to speak up or to keep my own counsel?

What do I want more of/less of in my life?

Affirmations

I already have all the answers I need inside of me.

I trust my intuition.

Snapshot

The High Priestess

Riffling through
your soul's cache:
seeing all the secrets

3 The Empress

Nurturing and Boundaries

Drawing the Empress may indicate that you are being called to give more to others than you have in the past. Just as a mother makes personal sacrifices for her children, so you may be asked to give up something in order to nurture someone else. In contrast, drawing the Empress may indicate that you have not been practicing the self-care you need, that you have placed others' needs too far ahead of your own. When that is the case, the message of this card is to gently disentangle from those situations and set necessary boundaries. Drawing the Empress can also signal a time of intense creativity. You may feel compelled to express yourself artistically. This may be minimal – adding flourishes to work you already do – or life changing – embarking on a new venture. The Empress energy is strong; be sure to carefully consider the whole picture before making major changes.

Dark Side

The Empress can give to the point of self-depletion and resentment, sacrificing her mental or physical wellbeing. Sometimes this is an ongoing pattern, reflecting a model of behavior that was taught in childhood. In that case, a person may need the help of a therapist or counselor to change these self-destructive patterns.

Light Side

The archetypal *earth mother,* the Empress is a lover, a goddess. She is sensual, perhaps even hedonistic. When you draw this card, look for ways to bring more sensual enjoyment into your life, perhaps through satisfying sex or delicious food, perhaps through new music or art, perhaps through massage or aromatherapy.

Between the Decks

Many decks show The Empress as pregnant. This is true for Tranquil Willows pictured here, Lover's Path, and Robin Wood. Waldherr's Goddess Tarot and Lover's Path name the card Fertility. Motherpeace includes a glimpse of the grain-goddess Demeter underground, also denoting fertility. New Vision shows young children behind the Empress' throne. Crowley's Thoth includes a mother swan with her ducklings. All these emphasize both literal and figurative birth – the Empress may be pregnant with a child, idea, or new project. Rider-Waite-Smith and Motherpeace emphasize the love-goddess aspect of the card, and Tranquil Willows, which includes a heart in the deep-red background, combines mother-goddess and love-goddess, showing that motherhood can be pleasurable.

As Lifetime Symbol or Name Symbol

A person with the Empress as Lifetime or Name Symbol is a giver. She is an earth mother, the ultimate nurturer (even if she is a man).

She is creative and sensual and often enjoys baking, gardening, and any hands-on creative work. She gravitates toward the helping professions. An Empress is a thoughtful lover and knows how to take care of others. However, she has a very hard time taking care of herself or allowing others to take care of her. She always has an ear to listen and a shoulder to cry on but may have difficulty opening up her inner thoughts and emotions to others. Appropriate self-care and boundaries are two main challenges of Empresses. See the *Numerology* chapter for a discussion of symbols.

As Year Symbol

The Empress year brings creative projects and self-care. The challenge of people in an Empress year is to examine their own flow of energy, to notice how many of their activities nurture them or drain them, and to revise their schedules accordingly. Often a small change, such as Sunday mornings to spend as they wish or an evening art class, can make a big difference in their outlook and energy level. People in an Empress year must take care of themselves or face the consequences: poor health, depression, disintegrating relationships. Their main task may well be to set healthy boundaries with themselves and others. See the *Numerology* chapter for a discussion of symbols.

In Spiritual Work

The Empress can be used in spiritual work. Try accessing your creativity through the meditation exercises in the last chapter of this book using the Empress card as a focus. This card can also be used to draw creative energy into your life via prayer or ritual. Lay the Empress on your altar along with the Three that embodies what you need most: the Three of Discs to develop your skills with the help of others or to receive more recognition from others for your work; the Three of Swords for art therapy, to use your creativity to heal from past hurts; the Three of Wands to attract more creative opportunities; or the Three of Cups to connect with love and friendship via your projects. See the *Tarot for Meditation and Spiritual Intent* chapter for further discussion.

Questions to Ask

Do I allow others to give to me as much as I give to them?

Do I nurture myself as much as I nurture others?

Do I take more than I give?

Affirmations

I revel in the sensual enjoyments of the day.

I express myself creatively.

I practice self-care today.

Snapshot

The Empress

Teeth sink
into warm bread:
olive oil glistens on lips

4 The Emperor

Authority and Achievement

Traditionally, the Emperor portends career success. Drawing this card signals that earning recognition, a raise, a promotion, or a new position is likely at this time. The Emperor is an authority figure. He may be calling you to step up into a stronger leadership position – at work, in your family, or in your community. In personal interactions, others will listen to what you have to say, but there is a caution to not be too overbearing. Just like any seasoned ruler, the Emperor must use his power wisely. When the Emperor represents a boss or someone in a position of power, don't challenge that person. You will not win. When the Emperor represents someone close to you, know that fighting stubbornness with stubbornness is generally self-defeating. Focus on what the other person wants and what you want, and look for creative ways to achieve an acceptable compromise.

Dark Side

The Emperor is a Type A personality. He thrives and excels in a fast-paced, stressful environment. However, ceaseless exertion of this kind has a high cost in mental and physical health and in personal relationships. Drawing this card may indicate that you need to slow down and examine your work/life balance.

Light Side

If you were going to a costume ball as a famous ruler, male or female, whom would you choose? Your choice can be revealing. For example, if you choose Mary Queen of Scots, perhaps you would like to feel free to "lose your head," or behave wildly, a bit more often.

Between the Decks

Motherpeace and Tranquil Willows pictured here emphasize the ego-driven alienation of the Emperor as one isolated in his position of authority. Robin Wood emphasizes the calm, confident authority of a leader who wears his mantle of power lightly. Crowley's Thoth and New Vision emphasize the burden of power held by one who can handle the weight. Thoth and New Vision both reveal the animal-wisdom available to these leaders – two rams in Thoth and an eagle and tortoise in New Vision. Waldherr names this card Power in both Lover's Path and Goddess Tarot. Lover's Path depicts a male and female sovereign ruling side-by-side, emphasizing the need for balance.

As Lifetime Symbol or Name Symbol

A person with the Emperor as Lifetime or Name Symbol is a leader. He is a father figure, a protector and provider (even if he is a woman). He is a natural authority who can easily command attention and respect. He has a swift insight into strategic problems and an excellent sense of politics. The Emperor is usually very successful in his career. He encounters frequent problems in his personal life, however, because he is often plagued by ego-based fears. He has difficulty getting in touch with his true feelings and making himself vulnerable to others. See the *Numerology* chapter for a discussion of symbols.

As Year Symbol

For people who are not natural leaders, the Emperor year challenges them to become comfortable with their own power and authority. This year they may find themselves in leadership positions they did not seek, and they may be forced to stand up for themselves in situations where they would normally give in. For people who are comfortable being in charge, the Emperor year challenges them to temper their authority with compassion. They may be forced to consider the needs of others in ways that they usually don't, and they may be challenged to open up emotionally to someone else. See the *Numerology* chapter for a discussion of symbols.

In Spiritual Work

The Emperor can be used in spiritual work. Try accessing your potential for success in a certain situation through the meditation exercises in the last chapter of this book using the Emperor card as a focus. This card can also be used to draw more success into your life via prayer or ritual. Lay the Emperor on your altar along with the Eight of Wands (swiftness), the Ace of Wands (oomph), the Ten of Discs (money), the Six of Discs (success), and the Three of Discs (recognition from others). See the *Tarot for Meditation and Spiritual Intent* chapter for further discussion.

Questions to Ask

Do I err on the side of being overbearing or on the side of not speaking up enough? What changes do I need to make in this area of my life?

Have I taken on too much leadership or not enough? Am I too driven or not driven enough? What changes do I need to make in my career and personal life?

Affirmations

I speak with power and authority.

I listen to others with empathy.

I prioritize a healthy work/life balance.

Snapshot

The Emperor

A whiff of Clive Christian No. 1
the silent purr of his
Bentley Continental

5 The Hierophant

Security and Conformity

The Hierophant often appears when we are longing for a sense of security, when we are torn between conventional vs. unconventional choices, or when we are feeling judgmental or judged. The Hierophant, or high priest, often gets entangled in the letter of the law rather than the spirit of the law. Yet the Hierophant has tasted spiritual mysteries. He has come into numinous contact with the divine during mass. This card reminds us that we all have the ability to do the same. The Hierophant advises you to move the discussion out of your head and into your heart. Whether you are seeking or resisting commitment, debating whether to play it safe or take a risk, or wrestling with what should or shouldn't be done, this is not a problem you can think your way through. When drawn with the Eight or Nine of Swords, the message is that you are not seeing clearly.

Dark Side

The Hierophant can represent a charlatan or warn of fraud. This especially applies to religious leaders, healers, advisors, and teachers. Drawing this card can serve as a warning to carefully check the person's credentials before becoming involved with him. It may also indicate that a person or product is a shallow imitation of an original.

Light Side

Drawing the Hierophant provides an excellent opportunity to release outdated beliefs, especially beliefs about what we can't or shouldn't do. The next time an inappropriate "can't" or "shouldn't" pops into your mind, talk back to it with authority – "Oh yes I can! Certainly I should!" – and proceed to do just that.

Between the Decks

Tranquil Willows pictured here and Motherpeace show the Hierophant as religious charlatan, as discussed in *Dark Side* above. Tranquil Willows raises the specter of Jim Jones and the mass suicide that resulted from his leadership of the People's Temple. Motherpeace harks back to the time male priests usurped the role of female priestesses. Conversely, Crowley's Thoth shows the Hierophant in communion with deep spiritual mysteries. Rider-Waite-Smith, New Vision, and Robin Wood emphasize the conventional Judeo-Christian aspects of the Hierophant's role. Waldherr names this card Tradition in both Lover's Path and Goddess Tarot. The goddess Juno represents the inherent power and security of marriage in Goddess Tarot.

As Lifetime Symbol or Name Symbol

A person with the Hierophant as Lifetime or Name Symbol is a critic. At his worst, he is plagued by self-criticism which he may project onto others, feeling especially irritated with those who break social mores. He often feels torn between security and freedom, between traditional structures and alternative lifestyles. The Hierophant's challenge is to work through his own fears and doubts, to give himself permission to be who he is. This is often accomplished through deep spiritual study or ongoing work with a therapist. Once he makes peace with his true desires, he is able to be a beacon, even a spiritual leader, for others. See the *Numerology* chapter for a discussion of symbols.

As Year Symbol

The Hierophant year often brings a longing for security. People in a Hierophant year feel a strong pull to honor tradition in the areas of family, love-relationships, religion, culture, or career. Conversely, they may be challenged to examine the reasons they have broken away from tradition. People in a Hierophant year may also be faced with judgmentalisim – theirs towards others and others' towards them. These issues can be worked out through regular journaling and meditation or with the help of a trained teacher. As they gain insights about themselves, they may be called to help others with similar struggles. See the *Numerology* chapter for a discussion of symbols.

In Spiritual Work

The Hierophant can be used in spiritual work. Try exploring your desire for security through the meditation exercises in the last chapter of this book using the Hierophant card as a focus. This card can also be used to draw more security into your life via prayer or ritual. Lay the Hierophant on your altar along with the Four that embodies the ways you want to feel more secure: the Four of Discs to feel more financially secure or more secure in your home; the Four of Swords to feel more peaceful and secure in your thoughts; the Four of Wands to feel more secure in your relationships; or the Four of Cups to feel more secure in your choices, especially about saying *no*. See the *Tarot for Meditation and Spiritual Intent* chapter for further discussion.

Questions to Ask

What would make me feel more secure? What has made me feel secure in the past?

Would the social ease and security of a conventional choice outweigh the freedom of an unconventional choice? What does my heart want?

In what ways have I been judged? In what ways am I judging others? What changes can I effect in these situations?

Affirmations

I cultivate the security I need.

I am at peace with my choices.

I give others permission to make their own choices.

Snapshot

The Hierophant

Relief:
closing the door
turning the lock

6 The Lovers

Relationship and Wholeness

The Lovers card is often about romantic partnerships, and drawing the card in response to a relationship question can indicate the beginning of a new attachment or the deepening of an existing one. This card represents soul mates, people with a deep, lasting connection to each other, not just casual partners. Drawing the card in response to a question about yourself indicates a need to bring more passion into your life via activities and connections that feed the soul. The time may be right to be more open about a previously private area of your life. The time may be right to become more publically involved in a pursuit or cause that you have previously kept quiet about. The time may be right to reconcile your outward behavior with your inner values. Whether you are in a relationship or not, the Lovers is about becoming whole, about bringing a sense of completeness to our often-fragmented lives.

Dark Side

When you are immersed in an all-encompassing relationship, drawing the Lovers can warn against codependency. Whether you are at the height of a new passion or experiencing relationship pain, this card reminds you to not lose yourself in another. This card advises you to practice self-care by maintaining independent friendships, interests, and activities.

Light Side

Sometimes drawing the Lovers counsels you to become a better lover to yourself, to do for yourself what you wish others would do for you. This can be as simple as buying yourself a desired gift and booking a massage, or as complex as exploring the full range of your sexual desires.

Between the Decks

Rider-Waite-Smith, Robin Wood, and Tranquil Willows pictured here portray a nude male-female couple in a Garden of Eden setting. Cosmic Tribe includes three Lovers cards: male-male, male-female, and female-female. All these decks emphasize sexual partnership. Motherpeace, Crowley's Thoth, and Waldherr's Lover's Path emphasize marriage and soul mates. Waldherr's Goddess Tarot emphasizes love as a force via the goddess Venus. The Hermit standing behind the couple in Crowley's Thoth reminds lovers of Rumi's advice to "let the winds of heaven dance" between them, reminds them to maintain their separate selves even as they join together.

As Lifetime Symbol or Name Symbol

A person with the Lovers as Lifetime or Name Symbol is a unifier. She brings a spirit of cooperation and sense of identity to her family, friends, lovers, and coworkers. She draws people together into groups and infuses those groups with a sense of purpose and passion. Her challenge is to experience that same sense of unity in her own life, which tends to feel fragmented, and to herself, which is often conflicted. A Lover tends to be strongly drawn to romantic relationships, and these relationships are often the breeding ground for her life lessons. See the *Numerology* chapter for a discussion of symbols.

As Year Symbol

The Lovers year often brings lessons around love relationships, positive and negative. People in a Lovers year may gain an important new love relationship, the revitalization of an ongoing one, or greater insights into past relationships. Their deepest lessons, however, are really about themselves. The challenge of people in a Lovers year is to bring about an internal marriage, to unify all the fragmented parts of themselves and their lives. Often this means coming to terms with conflicting needs and desires, both inside and outside of love relationships. Often this means coming to terms with their public and private selves. See the *Numerology* chapter for a discussion of symbols.

In Spiritual Work

The Lovers can be used in spiritual work. Try exploring ways you can attract or express more love through the meditation exercises in the last chapter of this book using the Lovers card as a focus. This card can also be used to draw more love into your life via prayer or ritual. Lay the Lovers on your altar along with the card that embodies what you want more of: the Ace of Cups for fulfillment and expression of love in any situation; the Two of Cups to attract or deepen romantic love; the Four of Wands for security and commitment in a relationship; and the Ace of Wands for more passion. See the *Tarot for Meditation and Spiritual Intent* chapter for further discussion.

Questions to Ask

In what ways do I feel fragmented? How can I feel more whole?

Is there an area of my life that I've been hiding, that I am now ready to be more open about?

What makes me feel loved and fulfilled?

Affirmations

I am capable of meeting my own needs.

I ask for what I want without shame.

I express passion and authenticity in my life.

Snapshot

The Lovers

Bacon and dark chocolate
wedded
on the tongue

7 The Chariot

Success and Self-Mastery

Drawing the Chariot signals that you are now ready to move ahead – in career, in creative projects, in relationships, and in personal growth. If you have been waiting to make a move – to a new city, to a new job, to a new relationship or lifestyle – the Chariot signals that opportunity is now open. However, advancement will not be handed to you. You must work for it. Such moves often require changing your thinking and behavior. Improving your self-esteem, finances, self-promotion, and daily self-discipline is often required. If you are feeling stuck when you draw this card, be encouraged, but be aware that you may need to overcome some internal or external blocks before you can move forward. Carefully examine what is holding you back and formulate a strategy to move past that. While seeking professional advice can be helpful, the footwork and final decisions must be yours.

Dark Side

Sometimes the Chariot appears when we are feeling out of control. If you have said more than you should, focus on "restraint of tongue and pen" – and restraint of the send key. If a person, situation, or your own behavior is threatening your physical or emotional safety, take the needed steps to extricate yourself.

Light Side

Drawing this card encourages you to travel for pleasure, as time and finances allow. Perhaps you've been postponing a desired trip with excuses, or perhaps you really are limited in the ability to get away. The Chariot reminds you that even a budget weekend at a local nature spot can be revitalizing.

Between the Decks

Tranquil Willows pictured here, Waldherr's Goddess Tarot, and Motherpeace show forward movement through force of will. Crowley's Thoth and Robin Wood focus on the meditative and creative forces moving the chariot forward. Waldherr's Lover's Path names this card Desire, emphasizing that our hearts will lead us where we want to go. New Vision portrays a darker message, showing slaves walking behind the charioteer, reminding the viewer not to be enslaved by someone with a dominant personality. Many decks emphasize the mythical aspects of this card via the animals pulling the chariot. Tranquil Willows depicts dolphins, Thoth and Rider-Waite-Smith depict sphinxes, and Motherpeace depicts winged antelopes.

As Lifetime Symbol or Name Symbol

A person with the Chariot as Lifetime or Name Symbol is a doer. He sticks with challenging tasks until he masters them, but is easily bored by monotony. The Chariot needs variety to stay sane and is happiest in jobs that offer him independence and daily challenge. He may have trouble sticking with long-term relationships, but with a compatible partner he can create a stable home life. The Chariot loves to be on the move. He chafes against any structure that he feels is holding him back. Travel is a favorite pastime, but he needs a strong center to radiate from. See the *Numerology* chapter for a discussion of symbols.

As Year Symbol

The Chariot year brings rapid progress. If people in a Chariot year have been waiting for opportunities to move ahead, those opportunities will open up this year. If some areas of their lives have felt stagnated, those areas will be revitalized. People in a Chariot year should be aware, however, that hard work and self-discipline are key to meeting their goals. Their challenge is to leave fears behind and to sit in the driver's seat. Once they do, success will follow them wherever they go. People in a Chariot year will be on the move in one sense or another. Travel of some kind is almost guaranteed. See the *Numerology* chapter for a discussion of symbols.

In Spiritual Work

The Chariot can be used in spiritual work. Try exploring the issue of self-mastery through the meditation exercises in the last chapter of this book using the Chariot card as a focus. This card can also be used to draw more self-mastery into your life via prayer or ritual. Lay the Chariot on your altar along with the Eight of Discs (self-discipline), the Queen of Wands (focus), the Knight of Swords (breaking away from bad habits), the Seven of Discs (patience), and the Three of Discs (cooperation from others). See the *Tarot for Meditation and Spiritual Intent* chapter for further discussion.

Questions to Ask

In what areas of my life do I feel stuck? What would moving ahead look like?

In what areas of my life do I need more self-discipline? What are some small steps I am willing to take right now?

Affirmations

I am in the driver's seat of my life.

I practice restraint of tongue and pen.

Snapshot

The Chariot

1950 Mercury Eight:
hydraulic lift
pearlescent flames

8 Justice

Karmic Lessons and Fairness

Drawing Justice about a current situation signals a return to karmic balance. Situations that feel wrong are about to be righted. Sometimes this brings loss, sometimes this brings victory, but nearly always this brings relief. Once Justice energy is in motion, you cannot exert your will to change the outcome, so the counsel of this card is to be patient and await more information. Drawing Justice about a future situation counsels you to consider the possible consequences before you act and to integrate the lessons of the past into future decisions. Justice may also denote legal issues and counsels you to fully research that aspect of any situation before becoming involved. Above all, Justice advises us to focus on *fairness* in examining our own behavior and the behavior of others. When Justice appears with the High Priestess or with a King, rest assured that you can trust your inner wisdom.

(Note: In many modern decks, this card often appears in position #11 instead of #8, but the earliest known decks place this card at #8.)

Dark Side

Sometimes Justice appears when you are going through a series of crises. When taken individually, these crises don't seem to have much in common. When examined as a whole, however, these crises may present an overarching lesson that can serve you well in the future. This is not punishment: this is how wisdom is gained.

Light Side

Numerous people need better advocacy: impoverished families, neglected children, abused spouses, the homeless, the developmentally disabled, veterans, LGBTQ teens, even mistreated pets. Many thrift stores are operated by organizations that serve one of these groups. Donating your material excess is an easy way to support such advocacy.

Between the Decks

Robin Wood, Rider-Waite-Smith, Crowley's Thoth, and Tranquil Willows pictured here include traditional symbols of the scales of balance and the sword of truth. New Vision shows the scales and suggests the sword by invoking the story of "The Judgement of Solomon." Waldherr's Lover's Path and Goddess Tarot depict weaving imagery instead, invoking the Fates. Motherpeace portrays the Fates, and Crowley's Thoth names this card Adjustment, emphasizing karma. Tranquil Willows' portrayal of the rising sun suggests the new day will be brighter. This rising light is also shown in Lover's Path, Goddess Tarot, and New Vision.

As Lifetime Symbol or Name Symbol

A person with Justice as Lifetime or Name Symbol is an advocate. She may be drawn to activist or legal work. She is focused on righting wrongs and empowering the disempowered. She often takes the role of peacemaker during a conflict but is willing to fight for justice as she sees it. She has more trouble, however, standing up for herself. Her personal life may include heavy karmic work in this lifetime. Sometimes a Justice person will seem to be caught up in a never-ending series of crises; sometimes she will appear to be incredibly lucky. Finding balance is a key challenge in her life. See the *Numerology* chapter for a discussion of symbols.

As Year Symbol

Any unresolved situation is likely to be resolved during a Justice year – legal, bureaucratic, or personal. People in a Justice year may experience some karmic realignment as what has *gone around* comes back. This realignment is something that happens without their conscious intervention. Attempting to control outcomes is futile here. As life unfolds before them, people in a Justice year are charged with simply making the best decisions in the moment. They may enjoy some wonderful rewards as well as some intense pain. Their ongoing challenge is to stay centered and to cultivate balance despite the highs and lows. See the *Numerology* chapter for a discussion of symbols.

In Spiritual Work

The Justice card can be used in spiritual work. Try exploring what is fair in a certain situation through the meditation exercises in the last chapter of this book using the Justice card as a focus. This card can also be used to bring about a fair solution via prayer or ritual. Lay Justice on your altar along with the King that best applies to the situation: the King of Discs for work and financial matters; the King of Swords for security and protection; the King of Wands for tricky negotiations; and the King of Cups for matters of the heart. To expedite a situation that is caught up in red tape, add the Eight of Wands. See the *Tarot for Meditation and Spiritual Intent* chapter for further discussion.

Questions to Ask

What is fair in this situation? Am I giving others the credit they deserve? Are others giving me the credit I deserve? Can an acceptable compromise be reached?

What is the lesson for me here? Is this similar to any of my previous life lessons? How might I do things differently next time?

Affirmations

I am at peace with my mistakes and imperfections.

I am worthy of all good things.

I have faith that justice will prevail.

Snapshot

Justice

Oakland, New York
Miami, Detroit:
out in the streets

9 The Hermit

Solitude and Independence

Drawing the Hermit often indicates a need for more solitude and independence. If the Hermit appears in response to a relationship question, one or both of you need more space. This doesn't mean the relationship needs to end. More time to yourself, a physical space of your own, and money that is yours alone are powerful remedies. These same solutions apply to caregivers of the ill, elderly, or young. These must be lifestyle changes, not one-time quick fixes. The Hermit lets you know that you cannot be passive here. You must take responsibility for your own life. This is especially true when someone is exerting too much influence over you. The Hermit often appears when we are facing life choices, especially choices that require a great deal of contemplation. Sometimes these are major life decisions, sometimes minor. Often the choices seem equally attractive or unattractive. When you still your mind, the answers will come.

Dark Side

If the Hermit represents someone else, you are encouraged to give that person plenty of breathing room. His withdrawal from you is not personal, not the result of anything you have said or done. Nor is his refusal of your advice an insult. This phase is simply a necessary part of his personal journey.

Light Side

How long has it been since you spent a few days entirely alone? The Hermit encourages you to spend some quality time with yourself – including unplugging from electronic devices. If this is difficult for you, spend a weekend in an area without access. Bring a journal and some uplifting music or books.

Between the Decks

The Hermit stands at the crossroads in Motherpeace and Crowley's Thoth and stands high on a mountaintop in Rider-Waite-Smith and in Robin Wood. The Hermit holds a lighted lantern in many decks, including Tranquil Willows pictured here. These portrayals symbolize looking ahead with wisdom, bringing insight to problems and decisions. New Vision and Thoth also include a serpent for wisdom. In Thoth it takes the form of an ouroboros, signifying the cyclical nature of life. The moon rabbit in Waldherr's Goddess Tarot represents the same. Waldherr names this card Contemplation in Lover's Path and Goddess Tarot; Tranquil Willows and Motherpeace name it Crone.

As Lifetime Symbol or Name Symbol

A person with the Hermit as Lifetime or Name Symbol is a loner. While he certainly enjoys the companionship of others, he needs regular solitude and a great deal of independence. If he lives with others, he needs his own physical space. He is a skilled listener and is often a wise teacher and mentor, but he limits his scope to one or two pupils at a time. In mythology, the Hermit is the keeper of the crossroads, and over his lifetime, he may be faced with a series of big decisions. With each decision, he gains more wisdom. See the *Numerology* chapter for a discussion of symbols.

As Year Symbol

The Hermit year brings reflection and decisions. People in a Hermit year will have to make regular time for solitude, even if they are in an intimate relationship or a caretaker of others. Such solitude is necessary for their peace and sanity. Like the High Priestess and Hierophant years, people in a Hermit year are charged with self-examination. They may be faced with a big decision. While others may offer help and advice, the decision is theirs alone. Hermits trust their inner-wisdom. This year is the end of the nine-year cycle and may bring a change of direction. See the *Numerology* chapter for a discussion of symbols.

In Spiritual Work

The Hermit card can be used in spiritual work. Try exploring the options in a decision you are facing through the meditation exercises in the last chapter of this book using the Hermit card as a focus. This card can also be used to achieve clarity about a decision via prayer or ritual. Lay the Hermit on your altar along with the Two of Wands (considering all the possibilities), the Ace of Swords (the truth of the situation), the Nine of Cups (what will make you happiest), and the Page of Cups (your feelings around the choices). See the *Tarot for Meditation and Spiritual Intent* chapter for further discussion.

Questions to Ask

Am I looking for someone else to fulfill a need that could be more appropriately fulfilled independently?

Am I too independent and not considerate enough of others? Do I include all stakeholders in my decisions?

How much solitude do I need? Do I plan enough in my schedule?

Affirmations

I give others all the space they need.

I take all the space I need.

Snapshot

The Hermit

No wifi, no signal:
the forest breathes
deep silence

10 The Wheel

Hidden Forces and Change

Greek philosopher Heraclitus noted that change is the only constant in the universe, and drawing the Wheel notifies you that change is coming your way. Sometimes this change is as natural and expected as spring turning to summer. When that is the case, you are reminded to reflect on the joys of each *season* of your life rather than complaining or resisting. Sometimes you have been actively working toward a change that has, perhaps, been slow to manifest. When that is the case, the Wheel indicates that events may be turning in your favor. Sometimes the Wheel denotes *fortune* in the monetary sense and indicates a change in your finances. Sometimes the Wheel denotes *fortune* in the sense of fate, signifying that hidden forces are at work behind the scenes. When this card appears with the Star, you are encouraged to have faith in a positive outcome.

Dark Side

Sometimes the Wheel brings unpleasant, unwanted change. At those times, it can be helpful to remember that loss, illness, heartbreak, and even death are inevitable in the human experience. At those times, it can be helpful to consciously practice gratitude for small joys and to do your best to be present and enjoy today.

Light Side

Consider your least favorite season. What are some small joys that time of year brings? For example, even if you loathe the cold, you might enjoy relaxing in front of the fireplace. Take some time to meditate on the pleasures of each season. Consider creating an art project along these lines.

Between the Decks

In most decks, this card features the image of a wheel. Imagery around the wheel indicates change. Tranquil Willows pictured here shows the phases of the moon, the seasons of the year, and the aging human face – traditional representations of the passage of time. Robin Wood shows changing human emotions. Crowley's Thoth, Motherpeace, New Vision, and many other decks use mythological symbols to indicate changes in fate and fortune. Many decks show creatures riding the wheel, commonly the sphinx on top and a demon on the bottom. Waldherr breaks from this imagery, naming the card Fortune which she represents as the goddess Lakshmi in Goddess Tarot and a visiting angel in Lover's Path.

In Spiritual Work

The Wheel card can be used in spiritual work. Try exploring the ways you embrace and resist change through the meditation exercises in the last chapter of this book using the Wheel card as a focus. This card can also be used to bring about positive change via prayer or ritual. Lay the Wheel on your altar along with the Ten that represents the area of desired change: the Ten of Discs for improvement in finances; the Ten of Swords to release the past; the Ten of Wands to complete a project; and the Ten of Cups for more emotional fulfillment. See the *Tarot for Meditation and Spiritual Intent* chapter for further discussion.

Questions to Ask

In what ways has change been positive in my life, both change I initiated and change I had no control over? How can I better make peace with change?

What, other than money, makes my life rich? How can I better savor these riches?

Affirmations

I embrace the joys of each season.

I accept change in my life.

Snapshot

The Wheel

Vanna White
gracefully turning
the winning letter

11 Strength

Inner and Outer Power

Strength often appears when we are in the midst of an ongoing difficult situation that requires fortitude of body, mind, and spirit. This card reminds us that we can always seek solutions. Stressful situations can be alleviated through vigorous exercise, extra sleep, healthy eating, and massage. You cannot perform well if your body's needs are unmet. Similarly, regularly taking short breaks, meditating, enjoying uplifting entertainment, and relaxing with friends also increase your ability to perform well. While these all take some effort, asking for help can be the most difficult of all. A powerful message of this card is that help, in some form, is always available if we ask for it and are open to receiving it. Sometimes this card indicates that we have more power in a situation than we are aware of. Drawing this card is an assurance that we have all the strength we need to do what needs to be done.

(Note: In more modern decks, this card often appears in position #8 instead of #11, but the earliest known decks place this card at #11.)

Dark Side

When this card represents someone else, it can indicate that she feels threatened by you or feels the need to threaten you with her strength. It may also indicate that she actually does have more power than you do in this situation. A wise strategy is to make her an ally if you can.

Light Side

Named Lust in Crowley's Thoth, this card counsels you to consider the positive manifestations of lust in your life. Sometimes when we lust after someone or something, we work harder to achieve what we want. Lust can provide that extra motivation to do what we need to, like showing up at an otherwise boring event.

Between the Decks

Many decks show a woman who has tamed a lion, as Tranquil Willows does here. The lion is a well-known animal symbol for strength and dominance. Rider-Waite-Smith, New Vision, and other decks show a beautiful woman closing a lion's jaw. Crowley's Thoth shows a naked woman riding the back of a multi-headed lion-like beast. She is clearly enjoying the experience and is clearly in charge. In both images, the woman seems to have tamed the beast through kindness rather than through cruelty. Motherpeace shows the naked goddess Bride surrounded by a variety of animal helpers. Waldherr's Goddess Tarot represents Strength as the goddess Oya controlling the wind.

In Spiritual Work

The Strength card can be used in spiritual work. Try accessing your personal power through the meditation exercises in the last chapter of this book using the Strength card as a focus. This card can also be used to increase your personal power via prayer or ritual. Lay Strength on your altar along with the Knight that represents the qualities you need: the Knight of Discs for more physical prowess; the Knight of Swords for more willpower; the Knight of Wands for more charisma; and the Knight of Cups for more emotional intelligence. See the *Tarot for Meditation and Spiritual Intent* chapter for further discussion.

Questions to Ask

What are my available resources? What are my strengths? How can I best utilize these?

Am I skilled at asking for help when I need it? Am I skilled at naming the specific help I want? How can I improve in this area?

Affirmations

I embrace my power.

I am willing to accept help.

Snapshot

Strength

One-armed woman
deadlifts
over 200 pounds

12 The Hanged One

Surrender and a New Perspective

The Hanged One appears when you are obsessed with something and have twisted yourself into knots trying to control the situation. This card invites you to turn a problem situation on its head. This requires a change of approach. Sometimes doing the opposite helps you step out of your usual role. If you have been strict, try being permissive. If you have been angry, try being relaxed or resigned. If you have been proactive, try practicing benign neglect. Sometimes all you need is a change of perspective to view a problem with new eyes. This can be achieved by listening to someone with similar experience, by viewing the situation with a longer lens or, conversely, closer up. Sometimes it helps to put physical distance between yourself and the problem situation, even if for a short time. Unlike the Death card, the Hanged One is not about grief. Instead, it is about relinquishing the illusion of control.

Dark Side

Sometimes this card signals that you need to let go of something you hold dear – an idea, a plan, a job, a relationship – especially if you have been trying unsuccessfully to make it work. This is especially true when the Hanged One appears in the House position of the Celtic Circle reading.

Light Side

Sometimes when this card appears, all you need is a pleasant distraction to give the issue a rest. Try playing hooky: sneak off to see a movie by yourself in the middle of the day, buy an ice-cream cone and eat it in the park, or dive into a fat, new novel.

Between the Decks

Most decks depict a figure hanging upside-down, as seen in Tranquil Willows here. Tranquil Willows, Motherpeace, and Robin Wood portray the figure as hanging from a tree branch in a relaxed way, invoking yoga or childhood play. Other portrayals are more sinister. Many decks, such as Rider-Waite-Smith, show the figure tied up. New Vision shows a jeering crowd below. In Crowley's Thoth, the figure is actually crucified upside-down. In Lover's Path and Goddess Tarot, Waldherr names this card Sacrifice. This imagery seems to originate in Norse mythology with Odin who sacrificed himself by hanging from the World Tree in order to gain knowledge.

In Spiritual Work

The Hanged One can be used in spiritual work. Try gaining a fresh perspective on a problem through the meditation exercises in the last chapter of this book using the Hanged One as a focus. This card can also be used to draw a new outlook into your life via prayer or ritual. Lay the Hanged One on your altar along with the Page that represents the area of your life that needs a fresh perspective: the Page of Discs for a fresh perspective on home, work, health, or finances; the Page of Swords for a fresh perspective on communication or ideas; the Page of Wands for a fresh perspective on spirituality or creativity; or the Page of Cups for a fresh perspective on love, grief, or over-sensitivity. See the *Tarot for Meditation and Spiritual Intent* chapter for further discussion.

Questions to Ask

What do I keep wasting my energy trying to control? What would happen if I stopped trying?

What are some positive ways I can *turn things upside down* in my life?

Affirmations

I relax into what is.

I surrender to the best possibility.

I embrace a new outlook.

Snapshot

The Hanged One

Loose change
falling
out of soul's pockets

13 Death

Endings and Transformation

The Death card signifies loss and endings – both current and past. This card also points to areas of your life that are in need of transformation. Sometimes this loss is an actual death of someone close to us. Sometimes it is the end of a job, relationship, home, or cherished plan. These losses bring grief, and one message of the Death card is to fully grieve what is gone. Sometimes this card asks you to revisit an old loss that is holding you back in the present. Drawing Death with the Chariot or the Sun encourages you to move on, to move out of the darkness and into the light. Drawing Death with the Hanged One may signal the death of a dream for the future and requires you to let go of what you thought *could be.* Moving through grief into acceptance and peace transforms our ability to live fully.

Dark Side

When Death is drawn in response to a question about a current relationship, the card suggests you let go of your ideas about what you thought the relationship could be, ideas you can now see are unrealistic. Death most often indicates a breakup, but in some cases couples are able to transform the relationship instead.

Light Side

Celebrating or borrowing elements from Dia de los Muertos – the Day of the Dead – can lighten the burden of loss with colorful altars for lost loved ones. Try creating an altar or art piece to commemorate a painful loss of any kind. Use photographs, candles, food, flowers, fabric, and religious or other symbolic items.

Between the Decks

Death is often represented by a skeleton. In Crowley's Thoth, he holds a scythe for reaping. In Rider-Waite-Smith, Robin Wood, and other decks, he holds a black flag with a white rose, symbolizing rebirth. A serpent symbolizes rebirth in Thoth and Motherpeace. Tranquil Willows pictured here shows the transformation of rebirth as a warm colorful doorway in the midst of a cold winter landscape. In Waldherr's Lover's Path and Goddess Tarot, this card is named Transformation. Lover's Path emphasizes the journey to the underworld through the story of Pluto and Persephone. Goddess Tarot emphasizes life-giving sustenance generated from death via the goddess Ukemochi.

In Spiritual Work

The Death card can be used in spiritual work. Try exploring ways to let go of something or someone through the meditation exercises in the last chapter of this book using the Death card as a focus. This card can also be used to help you let go via prayer or ritual. Lay Death on your altar along with the Five that represents the painful situation you are ready to let go of: the Five of Discs for loss of health, wealth, home, career, or loved ones; the Five of Swords for betrayal and hurt; the Five of Wands for conflict that cannot be resolved; or the Five of Cups for disappointment and lost opportunities. See the *Tarot for Meditation and Spiritual Intent* chapter for further discussion.

Questions to Ask

What old loss have I not fully grieved? How is that darkening my present? What would my life look like if I could let this go?

What hope or dream am I clinging to that has become unrealistic? What is my reality now? What would my life look like if I could let this go?

Affirmations

I give myself permission to fully grieve my losses.

As I let go, I make room for new blessings.

Time and distance bring relief.

Snapshot

Death

Marble monument
granite headstone
brass plaque: sprinkling of ash

14 Temperance

Balance and Flow

Temperance counsels balance, prudence, and moderation in all areas of life. Key to this balance is allowing your thoughts and feelings to flow freely, informing your decisions and inspiring you, but not overwhelming you. Temperance also counsels prudence in the flow of your activities: too much and you become exhausted; too little and you become stagnant. When Temperance appears in response to a question, the answer is to take a balanced, moderate approach. Avoid extremes: avoid reacting out of a heightened emotional state, and avoid shutting down. Staying present yet grounded when emotions are running high is a difficult task. Sometimes it is best to step away and redirect the flow of energy into a physical activity such as exercise, yard work, or housework. Whenever you draw Temperance, look for what is out of alignment and strive to restore balance. When Temperance appears with the Devil, look for problems of excess, possibly even addiction.

Dark Side

Aesop noted that fire and water make good servants but bad masters. Fiery emotions, such as anger and passion, and watery emotions, such as sadness and fear, can easily escalate out of balance and cause harm to self and others. Look for this when Temperance appears with one of the Fives.

Light Side

Physical disciplines such as ballet, yoga, Tai Chi, and martial arts can improve balance – not just physical balance, but mental and emotional balance as well. Yin Yoga and Tai Chi can be suitable even for people with severely limited physical mobility. Consider taking a class or following an instructional video in one of these arts.

Between the Decks

Waldherr's Goddess Tarot and Tranquil Willows pictured here emphasize the balance aspect of this card, while Motherpeace, Crowley's Thoth, and Rider-Waite-Smith emphasize flow. In Motherpeace, a shaman channels energy from other realms for her tribe. In Thoth an alchemist mixes fire and water. In Goddess Tarot, the goddess Yemana holds streaming water like silk. Many decks depict Temperance as an angel with one foot in water, one foot on land, pouring water from one chalice to another. In Robin Wood, this angel is juggling. New Vision adds air to the other elements represented in this card by including a hookah in the scene.

In Spiritual Work

The Temperance card can be used in spiritual work. Try exploring ways to bring more balance to a certain situation through the meditation exercises in the last chapter of this book using the Temperance card as a focus. This card can also be used to draw more balance into your life via prayer or ritual. Lay Temperance on your altar along with the Two that represents the area that needs more balance: the Two of Discs to better manage your schedule and To Do list; the Two of Swords to improve your mental balance and peace of mind; the Two of Wands to bring about a better work/life balance or social/solitary balance; or the Two of Cups to bring better balance to any relationship. See the *Tarot for Meditation and Spiritual Intent* chapter for further discussion.

Questions to Ask

> Where am I exercising prudence, moderation, and balance in my life, and where I am not? What small steps can I take to remedy these imbalances?

> Where is the flow of my life running too swiftly or too slowly? What can I do to bring my energy back into balance?

Affirmations

> Today I practice moderation in all things.

> I am proactive in keeping my relationships in balance.

> I channel my thoughts and feelings in positive ways.

Snapshot

Temperance

Dancing parallel
on tightropes:
Cirque du Soleil

15 The Devil

Projection and Self-Entrapment

The Devil represents what Carl Jung calls *the shadow*: wounded pride, selfishness, greed, and fear. This card often indicates that you are projecting your shadow onto other people and situations, creating problems where none exist. Often when this card appears, your own mind is the locus of your troubles. Perhaps a reoccurring nightmare or overwhelming emotion – worry, hurt, anger, regret – is the main issue you are facing. The Devil also appears when we have trapped ourselves by clinging to something harmful – perhaps to the point of addiction – or by reaching for what we cannot have. When the Devil appears with the Seven of Swords or the Hierophant, you are likely manipulating others to try to get your way. The antidote to all these painful situations is to get back to reality. The help of a trusted friend or therapist is often needed because our own views are distorted at this time.

Dark Side

When the Devil appears in response to a relationship question, one or both of you feels trapped. Sometimes this sense of entrapment is caused by a fixable problem or even a projected fear, but sometimes the problem is deeper. One or both may be tempted to sneak outside the bounds of your relationship agreement.

Light Side

The fears the Devil card operates through are often monsters formed in childhood that can't withstand the light of adult reason. Try this art therapy exercise: draw – or find a drawing of – a scary monster and write your fears around it. Hang this poster on your bedroom wall and laugh away its power.

Between the Decks

Tranquil Willows pictured here shows a naked figure chained near a treasure chest, but closer examination shows that the key is within reach, hanging on the wall. This theme of a chain one can slip out of is repeated in Robin Wood, Motherpeace, Rider-Waite-Smith and other decks, emphasizing that the Devil's entrapment is not real. Escape is always possible. In fact, the figures chain themselves through habit, greed, or fear. Waldherr names this card Temptation in both Lover's Path and Goddess Tarot, emphasizing that it is our own desires which entrap us. Crowley's Thoth portrays the Devil more positively as a psychological growth phase, depicting Rorschach ink blots and cell mitosis.

In Spiritual Work

The Devil card can be used in spiritual work. Try exploring your fear of being trapped through the meditation exercises in the last chapter of this book using the Devil card as a focus. This card can also be used to help you overcome your entrapment behavior via prayer or ritual. Lay the Devil on your altar along with the Seven that represents the behavior you want to overcome: the Seven of Discs to overcome impatience or lack of trust; the Seven of Swords to overcome manipulation or withdrawal; the Seven of Wands to overcome unrealistic demands or defensiveness; or the Seven of Cups to overcome unrealistic expectations, passivity, or fantasy. Lastly, lay the Chariot crossways over the top of your chosen cards to leave this behavior behind. See the *Tarot for Meditation and Spiritual Intent* chapter for further discussion.

Questions to Ask

What most triggers my feeling of being trapped? How has this manifested in the past?

When I feel trapped, how often has that reflected a situation I really did need to remove myself from? How often was it simply a fear projection?

How have I dealt, successfully and unsuccessfully, with feeling trapped? How can I improve in this area?

Affirmations

Fears are not facts.

I am willing to face what I need to face.

I take steps to overcome my self-destructive behavior today.

Snapshot

The Devil

Snooping his phone:
seeking
secret sexts

16 The Tower

Shake-up and Restructuring

The Tower represents dramatic or deep-level change that shakes up or even destroys your current situation. Sometimes this change comes from within after an experience that has completely changed your outlook, such as a lifestyle change after a health scare or a change of religious or political belief after a bout of disillusionment. Sometimes this change comes from without in the form of a car accident or natural disaster. When combined with the Emperor, the Tower can foretell an unexpected job offer that inspires you to change companies or even careers. When combined with the Lovers, the Tower can portend falling into or out of love and rearranging your life accordingly. When the Tower appears in response to a question about future choices, it can forewarn of danger on a certain path, allowing you to choose a different path and avoid the danger. Most often, however, the shake-up cannot be avoided. The Tower simply forewarns you to prepare yourself.

Dark Side

Whether you are on the active or passive side of a Tower shake-up, you may feel a strong desire to cling to the tatters of what remains. The counsel of this card, however, is that clean breaks are best. Be brave, walk away, and heal from your guilt or hurt in private.

Light Side

The destructive energy of the Tower is powerful. Destroying something (in a safe and reasonable way) may be healing for you at this time. Perhaps an old shed in the back yard needs to be demolished, perhaps some ugly old dishes need to be smashed, or perhaps some dusty love letters can be burned.

Between the Decks

A woman turns and walks away from the scene of destruction with only a light pack on her back in Tranquil Willows pictured here. In Waldherr's Goddess Tarot, a crying queen walks away from her tower holding only her crown. Both emphasize that at times it is best to cut our losses and walk away. Most decks focus on lightning striking and destroying a tower. Motherpeace shows the goddess Kali as wielder of the lightning bolts. Crowley's Thoth shows the Eye of God as originator of the destruction. The background of the Thoth card includes a dove with an olive branch, invoking the story of "Noah and the Flood."

In Spiritual Work

The Tower can be used in spiritual work. Try exploring an area of your life that needs to be restructured through the meditation exercises in the last chapter of this book using the Tower card as a focus. This card can also be used to help restructure an area of your life via prayer or ritual. Lay the Tower card on your altar along with the Ace of Wands for the energy this task needs, the Knight of Swords for the necessary force of will, the Three of Discs for rebuilding, and the Ten of Cups for satisfaction in the new situation. Lastly, choose a card from the *Minor Arcana* chapter of this book to represent the area of your life that needs restructuring, and lay that card crossways over the top of the cards listed here. See the *Tarot for Meditation and Spiritual Intent* chapter for further discussion.

Questions to Ask

In what situations in the past have I cut my losses and walked away? In hindsight, do I feel that was the best decision to make? Would I do so again?

In what situations in the past has the rug been pulled out from under me, leaving me stranded? In hindsight, how well did I cope with that situation? Would I respond the same way again?

Is there an area of my life that needs to be completely restructured? How can I go about making changes there?

Affirmations

I am fully capable of restructuring my life as needed.

I embrace the opportunity to start anew.

Snapshot

The Tower

2007:
Housing Market
Crash

17 The Star

Hope and Spiritual Connection

The Star card offers hope during dark times, reminding us that we can achieve our dreams despite all evidence to the contrary. The Star counsels you to connect with the *Source*, whether that source is God/dess, nature, or the love and support of those around you. The message of this card is to immerse yourself in whatever brings you the deepest sense of peace and wellbeing. The Star encourages you to have faith in yourself and in your future. As an artist masters her craft, she often goes through a developmental period where her product gets worse instead of better. If she gives up, she will never achieve her full potential. However, if she pushes through, she will emerge at a much higher level of mastery. The same is true in our personal development. Periods of failure can provide deeper lessons than times of joy, and we often emerge from those periods as spiritually richer, more compassionate people.

Dark Side

When drawn with the Hierophant, the Star can reflect a loss of faith. Sometimes this occurs as a result of alienation from or disenchantment with a belief system. Some people are able to return to that belief after a period of separation, but for others, the loss is permanent.

Light Side

Make it a habit to look up into the sky at night and find the brightest star. Use the childhood rhyme *"I wish I may, I wish I might, have the wish I wish tonight"* to strengthen a dream you are working towards or to regain hope during a dark time of your life.

Between the Decks

Tranquil Willows pictured here depicts a naked woman, under the light of an eight-pointed star, standing in water and pouring water over her head. Many other decks use the woman-star-water imagery. Rider-Waite-Smith and similar decks show the woman kneeling on land with one foot in the water, pouring water from two jugs. Motherpeace shows a woman submerged in a pool. It is raining, and a jug collects the rain. In all these cards, water is a soothing, life-sustaining force. The eight-pointed star represents Venus, and Crowley's Thoth shows the planet Venus in the background, emphasizing hope and love. Waldherr's Lover's Path names this card Grace.

In Spiritual Work

The Star can be used in spiritual work. Try exploring a situation where you need to regain hope through the meditation exercises in the last chapter of this book using the Star card as a focus. This card can also be used to draw more hope into your life via prayer or ritual. Lay the Star on your altar along with the Nine that represents an area of your life where you need to regain hope: the Nine of Discs to regain hope in health, home, finances, or family matters; the Nine of Swords to regain peace of mind and faith in your abilities; the Nine of Wands to increase your energy, sense of security, and spiritual connection; or the Nine of Cups to rekindle hope in love, happiness, or your life-long dreams. See the *Tarot for Meditation and Spiritual Intent* chapter for further discussion.

Questions to Ask

When in the past have I lost faith in myself or my future? What sustained me during those times? What was the eventual outcome?

How has walking through difficulties made me a better person?

What message would I give my younger self about faith and hope?

Affirmations

I have faith in myself and in my future.

My faith sustains me through the dark times.

Snapshot

The Star

Scores of Giselles:
the audition line
glitters

18 The Moon

Uncertainty and Unfolding

Drawing The Moon signifies that the road ahead is dark with no clear map to guide you. The outcome is unknowable from this vantage point. The counsel of this card is, as Lao Tzu says, to "let things flow naturally forward in whatever way they like." While this uncertainty often applies to outward circumstances – family, relationships, career opportunities, medical news – sometimes the uncertainty reflects inner change where you are surprised by a change of heart or mind, where you reveal yourself to yourself. Unlike the Tower whose energy is sudden and jarring, the Moon energy is calm and slow. This card encourages you to trust your future self to make the best decision at the time – right now you do not even know what the choices will be. Focus your attention on the present moment. Stay relaxed but alert. Forget about the destination, and be on the lookout for interesting and unexpected side-trips along the way.

Dark Side

Sometimes the Moon signifies that you are being deceived by an illusion. Remember that not everything that appears to be an opportunity actually is. The card encourages you to step back and look for places your attention has been misdirected. Examine the available facts. Proceed with a healthy dose of skepticism.

Light Side

How often do you look up at the moon and pay attention to her cycles? Since the beginning of recorded history, humans have looked to the changing moon as a metaphor for the changes in our lives. Try observing how these changing cycles affect your moods, desires, and sleep patterns.

Between the Decks

Most decks include an image of the moon on this card, but few include a photo-realistic moon as Tranquil Willows does here. The ocean, whose tides are ruled by moon cycles, also appears in many decks, representing both the individual and collective unconscious. Many decks feature a path between two towers, representing a journey. Rider-Waite-Smith and other decks suggest the journey begins in the water, leading to dry land or conscious choices. Conversely Tranquil Willows suggests the journey begins on land and leads into water, inviting the viewer to consciously explore her unconscious self. Motherpeace also presents this message. Waldherr's Lover's Path names this card Illusion.

In Spiritual Work

The Moon card can be used in spiritual work. Try exploring the truth and illusion of a certain situation through the meditation exercises in the last chapter of this book using the Moon card as a focus. This card can also be used to better distinguish between truth and illusion in your life via prayer or ritual. Lay the Moon card on your altar along with the Five that represents an area where you need to discover the truth: the Five of Discs for the truth about worry, finances, career, home, or loved ones; the Five of Swords for the truth about situations where you feel neglected, betrayed, or hurt; the Five of Wands for the truth about conflict or situations where you feel angry; or the Five of Cups for the truth about disappointment and lost opportunities. Lastly, lay the Ace of Swords crossways over the top of your chosen cards to bring out the truth. See the *Tarot for Meditation and Spiritual Intent* chapter for further discussion.

Questions to Ask

When in the past have I been faced with uncertainty? How did I cope with that? What would I do the same or differently next time?

When in the past have I surprised myself by discovering I had a change of mind or heart? Overall was that experience positive or negative?

When in the past has the process of unfolding been a pleasant experience?

Affirmations

I increase my tolerance for ambiguity.

I trust the process.

I trust my future self.

Snapshot

The Moon

Climbing the cliff path
at midnight:
flashlight goes out

19 The Sun

Vitality and Awareness

The Sun signals a time of renewed vitality: passion, good health, and joy. The Sun gifts you with all the energy you need to start or complete projects. If you have been experiencing hardship, drawing the Sun indicates the return of the light. Just as the sun brings light to the darkness, the Sun card counsels you to turn your awareness to the issue at hand. After some reflection, the solution will be clear. The Sun drawn in response to a question portends a positive outcome. Even when the situation looks dire, know that all will be well. When the Sun is drawn in combination with the Devil, rest assured that your fears are false. When the Sun is drawn with the Moon card, be encouraged that your dark journey will be short and will end in a pleasant place. Similarly the Sun ameliorates difficulties highlighted by other cards drawn.

Dark Side

Darkness can be safe and comforting while the glare of the sun can be dangerous. Sometimes this card brings up fear of exposure and vulnerability. Sometimes this card draws our attention to something that has been hidden from the light of day. Was it hidden appropriately out of a sense of privacy or hidden to deceive?

Light Side

This is a card of celebration, of child-like joy. Consider throwing an impromptu party in the sunshine around a barbeque, beach, or pool. Decorate with brightly colored balloons and streamers, and incorporate activities that made you happiest as a child. Invite both children and adults to join in. Don't forget the party favors.

Between the Decks

An image of the sun is included on this card in most decks. Tranquil Willows pictured here shows a woman peacefully enjoying the sun on her face. The Sun card often evokes a sense of celebration. Motherpeace shows a group dancing in the sun. Crowley's Thoth shows two children with butterfly wings dancing on a sunny hilltop. Waldherr's Goddess Tarot shows three goddesses dancing in sunlight. These are the Slavic Zorya who mark dawn, dusk, and night, emphasizing the natural cycles of life. Thoth also emphasizes these cycles with the Zodiac border of the card. Waldherr's Lover's Path names this card Awakening.

In Spiritual Work

The Sun card can be used in spiritual work. Try exploring how to bring more happiness into your life through the meditation exercises in the last chapter of this book using the Sun card as a focus. This card can also be used to draw more happiness into your life via prayer or ritual. Lay the Sun on your altar along with the Ace of Cups (overflowing blessings), the Three of Cups (celebration with others), the Six of Cups (what has brought you the most joy in the past), and the Nine of Cups (what you wish for most in the future). See the *Tarot for Meditation and Spiritual Intent* chapter for further discussion.

Questions to Ask

What were some of the happiest days of my life – both ordinary and special days? What made them happy?

When I feel sad, what comforts do I long for the most? How can I incorporate these comforts into my everyday life in healthy ways?

If I had unlimited energy, what would I accomplish? What does this tell me about my priorities?

Affirmations

I turn my face to the sun.

I allow myself to be happy.

Snapshot

The Sun

Emerging from
air conditioned darkness:
full glare in face

20 Judgement

Reawakening and Empowerment

Judgement often signals a time or reawakening where a part of your self or your life that has been dead is being revitalized. This can occur after recovery from a health problem, after leaving a job or relationship, or after losing a loved one or home. Sometimes the catalyst for this reawakening is clear, and sometimes it is not. Drawing the Judgement card can signal that a deep part of yourself has made a decision that you may not be consciously aware of yet. Only in looking backwards will you be able to see the point where you changed directions. Even before your direction becomes clear, however, the Judgement card advises you to trust your discernment. When Judgement appears with the Hierophant, you may be feeling pressure to conform to the values of others. However, Judgement encourages you to empower yourself to live by your own moral code.

Dark Side

When this card represents someone else, ask yourself whether or not you can trust her judgement. Look to her past decisions and behavior, noticing any times she behaved recklessly and endangered herself or others – physically, financially, or emotionally. Also look for any lack of discernment or intelligence reflected in her actions.

Light Side

Many beauty products and treatments promise *rejuvenation* which was once the realm of spirituality alone. Consider what makes you feel most rejuvenated and see what is available in your area. Whether you choose to indulge in a mud bath, a spiritual retreat, or a day on the river, take action to revitalize yourself.

Between the Decks

Robin Wood and Tranquil Willows pictured here focus on the phoenix as a symbol of rebirth, in contrast to Rider-Waite-Smith and other decks which focus on the Judeo-Christian idea of the resurrection of the dead for the Last Judgement. Motherpeace depicts a rainbow of light flowing from an ankh over the globe, suggesting that good judgement brings healing change to the world. Waldherr's Goddess Tarot shows a king kneeling before the triple maiden-mother-crone goddess, suggesting that the best judgement springs from a spiritual source. Crowley's Thoth names this card the Aeon and shows a seeker connecting with the spiritual wisdom of the ages.

In Spiritual Work

The Judgement card can be used in spiritual work. Try exploring ways to exercise good judgement in your life through the meditation exercises in the last chapter of this book using the Judgement card as a focus. This card can also be used to draw better judgement into your life via prayer or ritual. Lay the Judgement card on your altar along with the Queen that represents the area you need to focus on: the Queen of Discs for better judgement in the areas of health, wealth, home, and family; the Queen of Swords for better judgement in embracing ideas or beliefs, making decisions, and expressing your thoughts; the Queen of Wands for better judgement in priorities and passion; or the Queen of Cups for better judgement in love and expressing your feelings. See the *Tarot for Meditation and Spiritual Intent* chapter for further discussion.

Questions to Ask

What feels *dead* in your life? In what ways are you in need of revitalization?

What has made you feel revitalized in the past? Is that currently an option?

Who epitomizes *good judgement* to you? In what ways can you emulate that person?

Affirmations

I trust my judgement.

I live by my moral code.

Snapshot

Judgement

Green shoots
transmute
dead wood

21 The World

Triumph and Enlightenment

The last of the Major Arcana, the World reflects the wisdom we have gained since we started the journey as the Fool. Seeing with a god's-eye-view is one of the gifts of the World card. Sometimes this card appears when we are feeling on top of the world. Sometimes it appears when we are burdened by a world of trouble. In either situation, drawing the World reminds you to look at the big picture. When you are celebrating a triumph, the World allows you to see the terrain you have traversed to arrive where you are today, increasing your wisdom for tomorrow. When you are struggling with problems, the World allows you to see the way you triumphed over problems in the past, enabling you to better solve the problems of today. When the World appears in a reading, you are encouraged to look at the situation from a wider perspective.

Dark Side

Sometimes this card indicates greed – wanting the world rather than a fair share of it. Just like lust, greed can be a positive motivator, but also like lust, it most often exerts a negative influence. If someone is acting greedy when this card appears, see if a more reasonable compromise can be reached.

Light Side

The spectacular view of rising above the clouds in an aircraft at sunset can bring you a sense of peace and perspective that you can apply to a troubling situation. Consider a hike in the hills or a visit to a tall building to rise above the landscape of your life.

Between the Decks

The World is represented by a globe in Waldherr's Lover's Path and Goddess Tarot and in Tranquil Willows pictured here. More commonly the World is represented by a round or oval frame as in Crowley's Thoth, Motherpeace, Rider-Waite-Smith, and other decks. The blues and greens of planet Earth are common color schemes for this card. In Tranquil Willows the World is the belly of the goddess. In Thoth, turned sideways, it is the Eye of God. Motherpeace represents the central figure as World Mother with the children of the planet comprising the frame. Waldherr's Lover's Path names this card Triumph.

In Spiritual Work

The World card can be used in spiritual work. Try exploring a situation you need victory over through the meditation exercises in the last chapter of this book using the World card as a focus. This card can also be used to gain victory over a situation via prayer or ritual. Lay the World on your altar along with the Six that embodies what you need: the Six of Discs to gain victory over health, financial, home, or family problems; the Six of Swords to gain victory by removing yourself or moving on from a troubling situation; the Six of Wands to gain more recognition for your accomplishments; or the Six of Cups to gain victory over your emotions or over troubled love. See the *Tarot for Meditation and Spiritual Intent* chapter for further discussion.

Questions to Ask

How important will my troubles be months from now or years from now? What situations in the past mirror my current situation? What can I learn from those?

What perspective do I have today that I did not have five years ago? Ten, 15, or 20 years ago?

What makes me feel on top of the world?

Affirmations

I embrace a wide perspective.

Victory is mine.

Snapshot

The World

Apollo 17
capturing
the big blue marble

The Cards:

Minor Arcana

The Suits

The suits of the Minor Arcana correspond to the suits of playing cards, and both share similar origins in history. While playing cards are documented as early as the 10th century in China and India, the four suits we know today originated in 15th century France: diamonds (which correspond to discs), spades (which correspond to swords), clubs (which correspond to wands), and hearts (which correspond to cups).

In the Tarot, discs are also termed pentacles or coins and represent earth energy: the physical world, the body, and wealth. Swords are also termed arrows and represent air energy: the ego, the mind, and communication. Wands are also termed staves or batons and represent fire energy: passion, creativity, and sexuality. Cups are also termed chalices and represent water energy: the unconscious, emotions, and dreams.

Some readers find it helpful to memorize the qualities associated with each suit (above) and the keywords associated with each number (below). They can then relate these to the card image and more quickly access the card meaning for the Minor Arcana during a reading.

Aces

Gifts and Beginnings

The Ace of Discs

A giant hand offers a giant coin in the traditional representation of this card, indicating a gift, possibly wealth. Robin Wood and Waldherr's Lover's Path depict a secret garden, indicating a safe place to rest and grow. Motherpeace continues this theme with acorn imagery, reminding us that mighty trees grow from a small seed. Crowley's Thoth includes a cross-section of tree rings suggesting the passage of time. Tranquil Willows pictured here shows a solar cross engraved in a standing rock. This equal-armed cross within a circle is one of the oldest religious symbols, portraying earth, especially the four directions and the four seasons.

Drawing the Ace of Discs suggests the beginning of a new growth phase, one that will take some time to complete. Just as a young plant needs space to grow into, so do you at this time. Just as you clear space around a plant, water it, give it fresh air and sunlight, so must you care for yourself. Just as you cannot rush the growth of a plant, neither can you rush this phase. When drawn in response to a relationship or job question, this card counsels patience, care, and gentleness. Avoid expecting too much too soon.

The Ace of Swords

A sword accompanied by lightning descends from the clouds, in Tranquil Willows pictured here and in Waldherr's Lover's Path, indicating divine insight and truth. More traditional decks portray the same message with a giant hand offering the sword as a gift. In Waldherr's Goddess Tarot, the sword is stuck in the ground, reminiscent of Excalibur in the Arthurian legends, suggesting this gift is only for those worthy to receive it. In many decks, the sword wears a crown. In Crowley's Thoth, this appears to be a crown of light, depicting enlightenment. This message is also emphasized in Motherpeace which shows a yogi, surrounded by light, behind the sword.

Drawing the Ace of Swords encourages you to ask, "What is the truth?" This card counsels focusing on the verifiable facts. The underlying causes and potential outcomes are of no importance now. When this applies to yourself, it may be necessary to ask others to help you see more clearly. When this applies to someone else, look for any disconnect between what he says and what he does. His actions speak louder than words – especially at this time. Sometimes this card appears when you need to reexamine what happened in the past, to let go of your version of the story which may not be entirely accurate.

The Ace of Wands

A wand sprouting new leaves is offered as a gift in the traditional depiction of this card, indicating renewal. Waldherr, in her Lover's Path and Goddess Tarot decks, shows the wand planted in the ground. In Goddess Tarot, the wand is backed by the sun, suggesting a new day dawning. Fire imagery is utilized to show rejuvenation and passion in Robin Wood, Crowley's Thoth, and Tranquil Willows pictured here. Motherpeace emphasizes the life-giving properties of this card by illustrating a baby hatching from an egg surrounded by flames. Robin Wood also emphasizes this theme by including two sunflowers at the base of the wand, portraying this symbol as phallic.

Drawing the Ace of Wands reflects an influx of passion which can be channeled as reinvigoration, creativity, or sexual energy. Ask yourself what areas of your life may need an infusion of such energy. Where do you feel stagnated or bored – or in danger of becoming so? Drawn in response to a question about an existing relationship, this card suggests that the relationship needs more spice. Drawn in response to a question about a potential relationship, this card suggests strong chemistry and satisfying sex. Drawn in response to a question about a potential project or plan, this card gives a strong *yes*.

The Ace of Cups

An ornate chalice brimming over is the nearly universal image of this card, calling to mind the 23rd Psalm, emphasizing blessings and a full heart. Tranquil Willows pictured here portrays this message more emphatically than other decks by showing a waterfall running into and out of the cup. Robin Wood depicts a beautiful red heart within a crystal chalice. Connection with divine love is suggested in many decks. In her two decks, Waldherr includes the moon rising out of or descending into the cup. Motherpeace shows a figure swan-diving into an overflowing fountain. Crowley's Thoth includes a lotus flower, and traditional decks depict a dove holding a communion wafer.

Drawing the Ace of Cups suggests the gift of love, not just romantic love. Compassion, appropriate self-love, connection with the *Source*, and a renewing or deepening of familial and friendship ties could be indicated here. This is a healing love, a love that soothes and transcends. When drawn during a troubled time, this card counsels finding the emotional sustenance you need. When drawn during a happy time, this card counsels practicing gratitude and being emotionally generous with others. When drawn in response to a question about a potential relationship or friendship, this card counsels you to dive in.

Twos

Balance and Partnership

The Two of Discs

A juggler of two large spheres or discs creates an infinity symbol with his motions as we see here in Tranquil Willows. The figure eight of the infinity symbol signifies a cycle without end, such as the cycle of tasks in daily life. Both Crowley's Thoth and Motherpeace depict a serpent biting its tale, also emphasizing life as cyclical. Sometimes the juggler is also balancing on a wall, as seen above, or on a tightrope, as in Robin Wood, signifying the precarious nature of life and the need to walk through it with care. Thoth includes yin and yang symbols, further emphasizing balance.

Drawing the Two of Discs indicates that your hands are full. You may be feeling overwhelmed by schedules and commitments. This card often appears when we are juggling as fast as we can, moving from one task to the next with little reprieve. We may wonder if we are capable of sustaining this pace, and there is a caution to not to stay busy all the time. However, the figure in this card is fully competent, indicating that you are too. When this card represents a person you are frustrated with, do what you can to lighten her load instead of piling on more.

The Two of Swords

A woman dances with swords, emphasizing balance, in Motherpeace and Tranquil Willows shown above. Crowley's Thoth names this card Peace and shows crossed swords meeting in a lotus blossom, indicating peace of mind. Traditional decks show a woman blindfolded, shutting out distractions of the moment to focus within. Waldherr's Goddess Tarot and other decks set this card on a beach where land meets water, signifying balance between conscious and unconscious thought. In New Vision, a messenger approaches, suggesting that a clear answer will come soon. Waldherr's Lover's Path portrays this same message, showing a sleeping woman being visited by an angel.

Drawing the Two of Swords, especially in conjunction with the Five of Discs or Nine of Swords, indicates that your mind has been troubled and that you are seeking peace. Perhaps you, or the person this card represents, have been feeling mentally unbalanced in some way. This card can also appear when a problematic situation has no clear resolution. Set that aside for now. This card counsels you to engage in activities that will put your mind at ease. Rest assured that the solution will present itself in time. More thinking is not a good strategy now.

The Two of Wands

Tranquil Willows pictured above shows a Plains Indian wearing a buffalo-horned war-bonnet, emphasizing the ancestor-wisdom available through this card. Motherpeace indicates this message even more clearly with an African ancestor showing the figure in the card how to make fire. More commonly this card depicts a figure holding a globe and looking off into the distance, contemplating the future. Whether the focus is on the past or the future, the imagery in this card emphasizes pondering knowledge. Sometimes this card suggests a power struggle. Crowley's Thoth names this card Dominion, suggesting power used to subdue another. Tranquil Willows suggests power or knowledge used as defense.

Drawing the Two of Wands indicates the need for a plan and the need for a trusted advisor. This card encourages you to ask, "In what areas of my life do I need a better strategy?" Sometimes the best advice comes internally, out of prayer or meditation, sometimes externally, from a person or a book. When this card appears with the Five of Wands or Seven of Wands, it speaks to a conflict or imbalance of power. Have you been browbeating someone or allowing someone to browbeat you? This card counsels you to take the steps necessary to remedy that situation.

The Two of Cups

A modern couple toasts each other, in Tranquil Willows shown above, bringing up to date the imagery in traditional decks that depict a male-female couple in Renaissance garb. While the majority of decks portray a male-female couple on this card, the Gay Tarot shows two men, and the Wise Woman Tarot shows two women. Motherpeace shows the yin-yang balance of the couple through skin tone, cup colors, and the crescent moon, emphasizing the theme of emotional balance as strongly as the traditional theme of romantic love. Waldherr's Lover's Path shows two chalices on the ground next to an embracing couple. One chalice is overturned, indicating impetuous passion.

Drawing the Two of Cups indicates romantic love. Unlike the Lovers in the Major Arcana which suggests soul mates, the Two of Cups can apply to any romantic or sexual coupling, at any stage of a relationship. If this card stands for someone you are not involved with, it may indicate a hidden attraction – him towards you or you towards him. This is especially true when this card appears with the Moon or the High Priestess. Be aware, however, that he may have no intention of acting on those feelings. When the Two of Cups is drawn about a potential match, this card is favorable.

Threes

Connection and Expansion

The Three of Discs

Motherpeace and Tranquil Willows pictured here show three people cooperating to build something together – a home in Motherpeace and a backdrop for a ceremony in Tranquil Willows. Crowley's Thoth takes this theme further by naming this card Works. Three independent wheels connect together in a crystal pyramid, amplifying individual effort. The focus is on working with or for others. Robin Wood and traditional decks, however, focus on independent effort. They show a craftsman at work, gaining financial reward for his skills. Waldherr's Lover's Path and Goddess Tarot show a beautiful edifice already built, the results of the labor.

Drawing the Three of Discs indicates a project where you will be working with or for others – whether in business or in charity. Clear communication and cooperation are required. Respect for others is essential as is behaving in ways that will encourage others to respect you. Those working together were chosen for their expertise. Now is the time to show what you can do. If you are not currently engaged in a project, an offer may be coming your way. Sometimes this card appears when your work has been criticized. Whatever the case, the message of this card is that you can bank on your golden reputation.

The Three of Swords

Traditional decks show a red heart pierced by three swords, symbolizing emotional pain, often from a love relationship. Crowley's Thoth names this card Sorrow. Instead of a heart, Thoth shows a white lotus pierced by swords, referencing the Bible passage in Luke, "a sword will pierce even your own soul," since the white lotus represents purity of soul. This card also corresponds to depictions of the Seven Sorrows of the Virgin Mary, symbolizing emotional pain caused by family, especially children. Motherpeace and Tranquil Willows pictured here depart from this imagery, instead showing three figures in combat, indicating group conflict.

Drawing the Three of Swords indicates emotional hurt, sometimes oversensitivity. Traditionally this card reflects a love-triangle but can also apply to any combination of three caught up in conflict or drama. This card counsels careful examination – perhaps you are imagining a betrayal where there is none, or perhaps a group dynamic is triggering your own issues. If the problem is real, determine how you can resolve it. Sometimes bringing the issue out into the open for group discussion is the best solution, but other times it is best to take a break, postpone some plans, and give the situation time to settle out on its own.

The Three of Wands

A figure stands on the shore looking out into the harbor in traditional decks. He has sent off his ships and is excited to discover what they will bring back to him. His work is in progress but not yet complete. Motherpeace and Tranquil Willows shown above break away from this depiction. Emphasizing creativity, they show a mother engaged in art projects with her young children whose skills are in the process of developing. Crowley's Thoth depicts the dynamism of group energy, showing three wands crossed in front of a fiery background. All these illustrations suggest opportunity and exploration of new territory.

Drawing the Three of Wands encourages you to continue what you have begun and to be patient for the next phase to begin. Most of all, however, this card indicates new opportunities. You may need to exercise creative thinking in order to see what's right in front of you. You may need to come up with creative solutions in order to take advantage of those opportunities. This is especially true when this card is drawn with the Magician. When the Three of Wands represents someone else in a reading, she may be able to lead you to those opportunities or assist you in the completion of your work.

The Three of Cups

Three women toast each other in a circle on a sunny lawn in the traditional depiction of this card. Robin Wood shows the women in an ecstatic dance. Motherpeace and Tranquil Willows pictured here show the figures as nude or partially nude, suggesting they are engaging in ritual. Motherpeace furthers this ritual theme by including snakes in the dance. This is the card of friendship and of celebration, suggesting a harvest feast. Rider-Waite-Smith shows pumpkins on the ground, and Crowley's Thoth names this card Abundance. Waldherr's Goddess Tarot depicts the women at different ages, symbolizing the maiden-mother-crone and the cycle of human life.

Drawing the Three of Cups reminds you to enjoy your connection with others. When drawn in times of stress, this card recommends a night out with friends, time to laugh and be young again with those who know you best. When drawn in times of turmoil or uncertainty, this card suggests you take pleasure in your life. This is especially true when the Three of Cups is drawn with the Wheel – reminding you that what is down will be up again. The Three of Cups may indicate an upcoming celebration, possibly a baby shower or other multi-generational gathering. No matter what your situation, this card prescribes practicing gratitude for the abundance in your life.

Fours

Security and Rest

The Four of Discs

A king holds tightly to his wealth in traditional depictions of this card. Robin Wood and New Vision show this miserly attitude as isolating, illustrating the walls closing in around the king. Crowley's Thoth presents the opposite view, naming this card Power and showing a castle stronghold. A sense of privacy and safety permeate other decks. Waldherr's Lover's Path, Motherpeace, and Tranquil Willows pictured here show a female figure in a comfortable room. In Motherpeace, the woman is closing the door, shutting out the world. In Tranquil Willows, she is putting away a prized possession in her trunk.

Drawing the Four of Discs indicates a need for increased privacy and safety in your physical space. This is especially true when drawn with the King of Swords. The Four of Discs counsels making changes in your physical environment that allow you to feel more peaceful. This could be as simple as decluttering or as complex as installing a security system. Sometimes this card reflects a desire to clear your calendar and spend some quality time at home. This may stem from a need to remove yourself from harm's way or may stem from a feeling of being overwhelmed and undernourished.

The Four of Swords

A recumbent stone effigy of a knight on his tomb is the central image in most traditional decks. New Vision shows a corpse on top of his casket, while Waldherr's Goddess Tarot shows a live person sleeping. In all these decks, the main message communicated is rest, whether eternal or temporary. Most portrayals of this card are peaceful. Motherpeace and Tranquil Willows pictured here show a woman in sitting meditation. In Motherpeace, she sits within a golden pyramid of light. In Tranquil Willows she sits within a pentacle. Crowley's Thoth names this card Truce. In all these portrayals, mental detachment is emphasized.

Drawing the Four of Swords strongly indicates that you need a rest, especially a mental rest. Sometimes we must pose the extreme question – "Will any of this matter after I'm dead?" – in order to achieve the needed mental separation. When drawn with the Ten of Wands, the Four of Swords suggests you take a vacation from work. When drawn with the Three or Five of Swords, the Four recommends separating yourself from the cause of hurt. Sometimes this card appears when you need to recuperate after a time of ill health or after an emotional strain. Forced rest is never fun, but it is required in order to fully recover.

The Four of Wands

Many decks show a couple under a wedding canopy, indicating marriage. In some decks, like Robin Wood and Waldherr's Goddess Tarot, the couple dances. In some, like Waldherr's Lover's Path, they kiss. In others they simply wave at the gathered assembly. In Tranquil Willows shown above, a Maypole is being woven in an intricate dance. In Motherpeace, a group dances with garlands. Crowley's Thoth names this card Completion and depicts four wands forming a wheel: each wand has a dove at one end and a ram's head at the other, signifying a balance of masculine and feminine energy. Flames radiate from the center where the wands meet.

Drawing the Four of Wands in response to a relationship question indicates stability and security in the relationship, a long-term commitment. Sometimes this card portends a wedding. Couples are reminded, however, that marriage marks the beginning of a journey together, not the end. In times of trouble, this card reminds you to honor your commitment and to work out the problems. When this card appears outside the context of a relationship, it reminds you to be complete unto yourself, similar to the Lovers card described in *Major Arcana* above. It could also indicate the celebration of a milestone in your life.

The Four of Cups

Four chalices are the focal point in most depictions of this card. Traditional decks show three cups lined up the ground in front of a young man sitting under a tree. A fourth cup is floating in air, but the figure resolutely ignores it or doesn't notice it. The figure in Waldherr's depictions of this card is a young woman. In Goddess Tarot, she has her eyes closed in meditation. In Lover's Path she appears to be thinking. There are no floating cups. In Tranquil Willows pictured here, all the cups are floating above a woman's head. She appears to see them, but is not giving them much attention.

Drawing the Four of Cups indicates your choice of *none of the above*. Others may be pushing you to make a certain choice, but you are uninterested. Similar to the Four of Swords, this can be a restful card, a time-out from doing or deciding. When drawn with the Hermit, the Four of Cups emphasizes that the decision must be yours alone, made only after much contemplation. When drawn with the Hierophant, the choice may be between conventional and unconventional paths. The Four of Cups assures you that more information, and perhaps more choices, will be revealed in the future.

Fives

Suffering and Strife

The Five of Discs

Traditional decks show two beggars outside a church in a snowstorm, suggesting poverty, ill health, and being shut out of a warm sanctuary. Tranquil Willows pictured here echoes this theme, adding tears of pain or desperation to the beggar's face. New Vision and Waldherr's Lover's Path include an infant in the arms of the beggar. In these depictions, the five discs appear in the church's stained glass window, representing unattainable comfort and wealth. Motherpeace and Crowley's Thoth soften the pain of this card. Thoth names this card Worry, and Motherpeace shows a tense woman kneading bread, suggesting we work through our worries via physical activity.

Drawing the Five of Discs can point to health or financial problems. Sometimes the stress of worry is ruining your health. This card can also indicate that you feel excluded from a situation that previously brought you joy. Perhaps this exclusion stems from a lack of funds or from the physical limitations of illness that curtail your ability to participate. This exclusion may, however, originate from other people's attitudes and actions. You may feel shut out from an opportunity at work, from a circle of friends, from family activities, or from closeness in a love relationship. Consult the other cards in your reading for advice about how to proceed.

The Five of Swords

A woman points a finger at a distraught man, leveling an accusation at him, in Tranquil Willows pictured here. She seems to be calling him to account for his actions with the swords. More traditional decks show a figure gathering up the swords of the defeated on a battlefield. In Robin Wood, the young man taking the swords is clearly taunting the losers. In both Motherpeace and Crowley's Thoth, the swords form a downward pointing pentacle. Crowley names this card Defeat, and Motherpeace includes a wasp in the middle, suggesting a painful sting. In Waldherr's Lover's Path, Psyche is being abandoned by Cupid, left only with the now-useless arrows of their spent love.

Drawing the Five of Swords points to a sharp pain that results from being accused, defeated, or abandoned. This card can also indicate a lack of trust, unfairness, and a need for self-protection. Unlike the disruption of the Tower, the disruption this card brings is usually minor and temporary. The blow harms your ego, not your life structure. The Five of Swords in the Past or Above position in the Celtic Circle spread suggests that an old experience or an imagined experience is intruding on the present. This can also be true when the Five of Swords is drawn with Death, the Devil, or the Nine of Swords.

The Five of Wands

Five people joust with long wands in traditional interpretations of this card. Motherpeace includes an erupting volcano and a phoenix in the background, indicating that this competition is serving to release pent up energy and will result in a restructured group. Crowley's Thoth and Tranquil Willows shown above present a geometric representation of the five wands. The central staff in Thoth is a kerykeion, the herald's wand, also suggesting change as the result of strife. In Tranquil Willows, the wands are shafts of wheat. Their circular movement suggests a wheel, indicating karma: "As you sow, so shall you reap."

Drawing the Five of Wands suggests a conflict is at hand, perhaps one that has been boiling for quite some time. Those who have felt unappreciated are demanding their due and will not rest until a satisfactory solution is offered. A competition between egos may be the basis of the conflict. Sometimes this conflict can result in a reorganization at work with new management in place, a restructuring of home life, or a shift in relationship roles and responsibilities. Unlike the Tower, however, where such change is dramatic, the Five of Wands suggests relatively minor change. Sometimes the conflict this card reflects is internal, such as angst over an upcoming decision.

The Five of Cups

An anguished figure stands next to overturned chalices in many representations of this card. Crowley's name for the card, Disappointment, emphasizes the central message. In Tranquil Willows pictured here, a figure looks out the window, away from the overturned cups, searching the night for other possibilities. In Waldherr's Goddess Tarot, the figure walks away. While three of the chalices are overturned, most decks depict two full chalices still standing, suggesting that all is not lost. In Motherpeace, the cups are filled with pearls, representing life's riches. Other decks show the cups filled with water or wine, representing emotional sustenance or life force.

Drawing the Five of Cups indicates that you are experiencing disappointment or that someone is feeling disappointed in you. Regret, loss, and despair also accompany this card. The Five of Cups counsels you to carefully examine the cause of these feelings. Are you holding onto the past instead of moving on? Do you need to forgive or seek forgiveness? This card recommends that you recalibrate your expectations to better match your own capabilities and the capabilities of others. The Five of Cups also encourages you to focus on the blessings you do have. What is in the full cups?

Sixes

Harmony and Success

The Six of Discs

Crowley names this card Success in his Thoth deck. Waldherr's Lover's Path shows a man offering homage, laying coins at a beautiful woman's feet. The woman sits in front of a snowy window, indicating reward after a time of travail. Traditional decks show a wealthy man with scales in hand, paying alms to beggars, emphasizing generosity. Motherpeace and Tranquil Willows shown above focus on healing rather than on financial success. Motherpeace shows a supine figure receiving a massage. Tranquil Willows shows a prone figure attended by three crones. A bowl of incense, a bowl of fire, and a bowl of water rest by her side. The moon, the sun, and a yin-yang symbol overhead complete the representation of the six discs.

Drawing the Six of Discs portends success of all kinds. The rewards that you have earned will be laid at your feet. This card reminds us to be generous, not just with our wallets but also in our hearts. When drawn about a troubled relationship, this card counsels you to give the other person the benefit of the doubt. What allowances can you give him that you would like someone to give you if you found yourself in a similar situation? When drawn about poor health, this card advises you to seek out the healing you need.

The Six of Swords

In most depictions of this card, a family or an individual glides off in a boat. The swords frame the sides of the boat, signifying moving on after a time of trouble. In Robin Wood, an invisible guide accompanies the figure in a swan-shaped boat, suggesting fewer difficulties in the future. Tranquil Willows pictured here shows a young man setting off on a quest, a sword tunnel marking his entrance into a new phase of life. Motherpeace shows six women in a circle, floating high above a landscape, their swords meeting in the middle. This depicts a sense of detached perspective, as does Crowley's card which he names Science.

Drawing the Six of Swords indicates a lessening of difficulties or relief from a worrying situation. This card recommends distancing yourself in order to gain a clearer perspective. When drawn with Death, you are counseled to make a clean break. When drawn with Temperance, you are advised to gently back off and reassess the situation later. When drawn with the Four of Cups, no action is required – the problem will lose energy and wind down on its own. When drawn with the Chariot, you are counseled to physically distance yourself, perhaps by taking a vacation, or even permanently relocating.

The Six of Wands

A victor enters town on horseback to the accolades of those assembled. In traditional decks he wears a laurel wreath, emblem of Olympic glory. In some modern decks, the rider is a woman, as we see with the jockey depicted in Tranquil Willows above. In Waldherr's Lover's Path, five of the wands are living trees. In Robin Wood, the champion wears and carries a sun emblem, signifying dominance and yang energy. Both Crowley's Thoth and Motherpeace depart from the horse and rider imagery. The four-armed goddess Shakti rides a six-spoked wheel of fire in Motherpeace. Flames spring from the joinings of six cross-woven wands in Thoth, which names this card Victory.

Drawing the Six of Wands reflects a victory – winning public recognition, obtaining a job or promotion, or achieving a goal. This card counsels you to enjoy but not abuse your moment of glory, advises you to be sporting and to treat your competitors with respect. Sometimes this card represents an internal victory that no one but you can see. Drawing this card may affirm that you have met a personal goal or that you have behaved well in a trying situation. When drawn with the Three or Five of Swords, the Six of Wands commends you for stepping away from the drama and avoiding an emotional vortex.

The Six of Cups

Traditional decks depict a young boy and girl in a courtyard garden where six chalices have been repurposed as planters for flowers. The boy hands the girl one of these flowering chalices. In New Vision, an old couple revisits this scene in memory, emphasizing nostalgia and innocence. Crowley's Thoth, Motherpeace, and Tranquil Willows shown above depart from this garden imagery, focusing on water instead. Thoth shows a fountain of six golden cups and names this card Pleasure. Motherpeace shows six figures riding an ocean wave on seahorses, holding their cups aloft, the rising sun behind them. Tranquil Willows shows a figure in a boat under the night sky, six chalices outlined in stars.

Drawing the Six of Cups indicates an exuberance of emotion, sunny or dark. You may feel depressed, perhaps lost in the nostalgia of yearning for a golden time when everything seemed easier. Or you may be high on life, riding a pink cloud. Whatever your situation, this card reminds you that feelings aren't facts. When drawn with the Ace of Swords or the Moon, the Six of Cups counsels focusing on the truth. When drawn with the King of Cups or Temperance, the Six of Cups recommends more emotional balance. When drawn with the Sun or the Nine of Cups, the Six of Cups encourages you to relax into pleasure.

Sevens

Conflict and Intention

The Seven of Discs

A pregnant woman waits in a garden in Motherpeace and Tranquil Willows pictured here. Her belly is likened to the harvest, nearly ripe but not quite. In Tranquil Willows she paces, showing her impatience. Neither a birth nor a crop can be rushed. Traditional decks show a figure waiting to reap what he has planted. Seven discs on the vine represent his almost-ready reward. These coins instead of fruit remind the viewer that the harvest may be monetary. In New Vision, an angel visits the waiting man, encouraging him. Crowley names this card Failure which may indicate a failure of timing if one does not have patience.

Drawing the Seven of Discs suggests that you will soon be able to harvest the fruits of your labors – if only you can wait a while longer. Now is not the time to give up or to make demands. Unlike the Three of Wands where the work is in progress, your work is nearly complete. What you have been working for will soon manifest. Pay attention if another Seven appears with this card. The Seven of Wands may indicate the need to defend your territory while waiting for the harvest, but the Seven of Swords cautions you against being manipulative or underhanded. The Seven of Cups suggests you start thinking about your next goal.

The Seven of Swords

A woman hiding a sword behind her back faces off with a man in Tranquil Willows pictured here. Perhaps this is a secret weapon to be used later, or perhaps she will stab him in the back. In Motherpeace, a fox sneaks into a chicken coop. In traditional decks, a figure slinks off with the swords. All these depictions emphasize treachery, manipulation, or underhandedness. Crowley's Thoth names this card Futility, indicating that there is no viable solution to the conflict. Other decks, such as Waldherr's Lover's Path, present this card in a more positive light, focusing on a figure withdrawing from conflict and gathering swords for self-protection.

Drawing the Seven of Swords indicates a fight that cannot be won. Sometimes this card reflects minor bickering where the only winning strategy is to remain silent. Sometimes, however, the conflict is a major one. There may be a temptation to manipulate or to backstab – or a warning that someone else is doing that to you. Sometimes withdrawal is the best strategy. When this card appears with the King of Swords, you are encouraged to protect yourself. When this card appears with Justice, know that the situation will be resolved without your further participation. When this card appears with the Sun or the Star, have faith that the resolution will be satisfactory.

The Seven of Wands

In most traditional decks, a man stands at the edge of a cliff defending his territory. New Vision shows angry combatants closing in on the defender. In Waldherr's Lover's Path, Siegfried battles a dragon. The sun creates a halo around Siegfried's head, suggesting divine power. Crowley's Thoth names this card Valour for the courage needed to defend oneself. Motherpeace depicts a tamer conflict, women competing with words to sway a group or to win a leadership position. Tranquil Willows pictured here shows a young man readying his defense with a wall of flaming wands.

Drawing the Seven of Wands reflects a situation in which you feel pushed to the edge, where you must defend your ground at all costs. These challenges may come in the wake of recent success or public recognition. While you will not be able to win everyone over, you are required to meet any challengers head-on. This card represents issues you cannot compromise on. That is not a viable tactic here. Important principles or your character may be on the line. When this card represents someone else, avoid challenging her unless it is absolutely necessary to do so. She will not back down.

The Seven of Cups

A figure contemplates the choices represented by seven cups: wealth, glory, power, love, death, evil, and the deep mystery of life. Some decks, such as Motherpeace, show a clear choice standing out among the rest; other decks do not. In Tranquil Willows shown above, the cups appear in menorah-formation. In Motherpeace, the cups are part of a fountain. The chalices often appear amidst clouds, and in Robin Wood, the figure is clearly daydreaming, emphasizing the message of being lost in oneself or in thoughts of the future. Crowley reflects what happens when this is taken too far, titling his card Debauch.

Drawing the Seven of Cups indicates careful consideration of all the options, perhaps to the point of fantasy, perhaps prudently in order to make the best choice. If you have recently gone through this process when the Seven of Cups is drawn, the message is that you have a clear vision to guide you. If you are still in the process of considering the options, this card counsels full exploration before you choose. The Seven of Cups can also indicate that you or someone close to you has been distracted by thoughts of greener fields and may be neglecting the demands of the present.

Eights

Challenges and Change

The Eight of Discs

In Tranquil Willows pictured here, a woman creates a quilt. Motherpeace shows women sewing, weaving and creating pottery. Waldherr's Goddess Tarot shows a woman painting. New Vision shows a master and apprentice engaged in stone-craft. Robin Wood shows a young boy woodworking, and Waldherr's Lover's Path shows a young man metalworking. The emphasis in all these decks is literally mastering a craft, and the discs portrayed in the cards are often the products of that craft. However an underlying meaning is mastering the self, as can be seen in Crowley's Thoth which portrays a flowering vine and names this card Prudence.

The Eight of Discs often appears at the beginning of a new career path, although it can also apply to a new art form, skill, or sport you are invested in mastering. Drawing the Eight of Discs encourages you to pursue your talent with single-minded effort. If this card appears when you are angry at yourself, turn that energy into determination and motivation. Similar to the Chariot, the Eight of Discs suggests self-mastery. This card encourages you to eradicate a bad habit or form a positive one. At times this card can represent a perfectionist or micromanager.

The Eight of Swords

A woman blindfolded, loosely bound, and surrounded by swords is the central image in most decks, including Tranquil Willows pictured here. Like the chains in the Devil card, the bonds in this card can be discarded. The woman can escape if she chooses to. Waldherr emphasizes this theme in both her Lover's Path and Goddess Tarot by showing a woman lying among the swords, not bound at all. Yet it is clear that the central figure feels trapped. Motherpeace shows a figure breaking swords against a brick wall while another escape route is possible, emphasizing a lack of vision and poor strategy. Crowley names this card Interference, suggesting that something or someone is interfering with our ability to live freely.

Drawing the Eight of Swords indicates that you, or someone close to you, feel trapped. Often this sense of entrapment stems from a limited vision. You may not be seeing the situation clearly or may not be applying the best strategy. Sometimes this sense of being trapped stems from real limitations in our lives. Those limitations may be posed by health or financial difficulties, or by work or relationship problems. The first step in freeing yourself is to honestly assess the situation, perhaps with the help of a trusted advisor. Then you can determine which action would be most successful in ameliorating the problems.

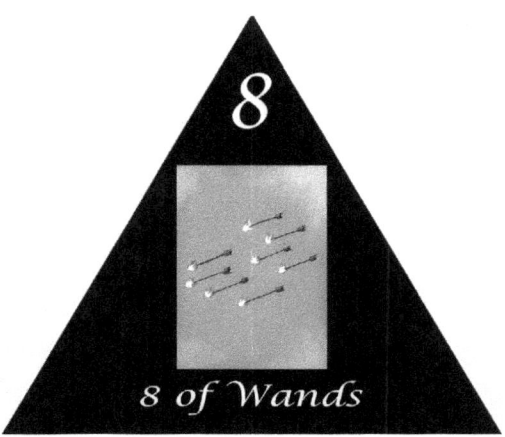

The Eight of Wands

Eight fiery arrows flying across the sky form the central image in both Motherpeace and Tranquil Willows pictured here. Crowley names this card Swiftness, and most decks show the wands in motion to emphasize that. Motherpeace shows a mythological creature firing the arrows, and New Vision portrays an angel. Both suggest a spiritual agency behind the movement: bringing a message, a new opportunity, or perhaps retribution. In Robin Wood, the planet Jupiter appears in the background, portending luck and good fortune. In Waldherr's Lover's Path, birds accompany the wands, promising hope and renewal. This message is also emphasized in Crowley's Thoth with a rainbow above the wands.

Drawing the Eight of Wands suggests a freeing up of energy. Anything that has been stalled will now either move forward or be jettisoned. This card suggests messages received, opportunities offered, and justice being served. Any obstacles that have been blocking your path are now cleared away. The whirlwind energy of this card can be a bit unsettling. You may be asked to travel on the spur of the moment, expected to work at a very fast pace, or be sucked into the vortex of a new project without time to fully prepare. Overall, however, the Eight of Wands portends smooth transitions into the next phase.

The Eight of Cups

In traditional decks, a figure walks away from eight chalices. His cloak and staff show that he is beginning a long journey. The traveler is now on the other side of the water from the cups, indicating his resolution to move on. New Vision shows fireworks in the background, suggesting the traveler is leaving drama behind. Motherpeace and Tranquil Willows shown above depict an inner journey instead of a literal one. In Motherpeace, an octopus holds eight unique jugs against a blue background. In Tranquil Willows, eight cups pour a rainbow of light onto a woman's head. Her eyes are closed in contemplation. Crowley names this card Indolence, reflecting self-absorption.

Drawing the Eight of Cups reflects a decision to withdraw. This withdrawal may be from an external situation – a job, role, friendship, or love relationship – or from the world at large. This card suggests that the situation you are withdrawing from is no longer fulfilling and that the time is right to move on. When the withdrawal is internal, this card may indicate depression, specifically a desire to hide away and indulge blue feelings. While taking time to process emotions is healthy, getting bogged down in them is not. At some point, action must be taken.

Nines

Reflection and Completion

The Nine of Discs

Crowley names this card Gain. This theme is echoed in many decks, including Tranquil Willows above which shows a merchant clutching his bag of gold. Traditional decks portray a woman in a secret garden, perhaps the same garden from the Ace of Discs. However in this garden, gold coins are growing on the vines, suggesting prosperity. The reflective quality of this card emphasizes that prosperity brings leisure. The woman holds a falcon on her wrist, signifying her access to higher vision. In Waldherr's Lover's Path and Goddess Tarot, a dove replaces the falcon, indicating peace. Motherpeace shows a solitary shaman completing a medicine wheel sand painting, depicting solitude for spiritual connection.

Drawing the Nine of Discs reminds you to take some time to refresh your spirit. You have achieved enough success to feel some security in your position, and the time off is well earned. When you draw this card in the midst of a busy time, remember that you can take a few hours to yourself here and there, even if you can't get away for multiple days. In fact, a regular time to meditate daily or weekly can be even more effective than a vacation. If you draw this card in relation to someone else, you are encouraged to allow that person the solitude she needs.

The Nine of Swords

A woman sits up in bed, hands covering her face in anguish, nine swords in the background. This is the image in Tranquil Willows above as well as in most decks. In Waldherr's Lover's Path, an angel tries to hand an arrow to the woman – indicating truth – but she doesn't notice him. She also doesn't notice the open treasure box resting on the table beside her. Motherpeace shows a woman lying on a bed of swords. Her astral body rises, holding a flaming sword with an eye in the hilt. She brandishes this sword to fight off the nightmare images which rise to greet her. Crowley names this card Cruelty.

Drawing the Nine of Swords indicates insomnia, nightmares, and a disturbed state of mind. The lesson of the Ace of Swords – focusing on the truth – has not been learned. The mental disturbance this card indicates is fear-based, not reality-based. However, this card does demand that we face and vanquish our demons in order to move out of this dark time, in order to achieve the surrender the Ten of Swords indicates. Often these fears are deep, formed in our youth. Often memories of a bad past experience have been triggered by a present situation, and we are both re-suffering the past and pre-suffering a projected future, being cruel to ourselves in the process.

The Nine of Wands

The four-armed goddess Shakti dances with nine lit torches in Tranquil Willows pictured here. A halo of light frames her head. Motherpeace shows a woman sitting in meditation, nine lit torches arrayed behind her, a spiraling snake on each side of her. Both portrayals suggest enlightenment and spiritual rejuvenation, a completion of the work begun in the Ace of Wands. Crowley names this card Strength, indicating the need to conserve our strength and expend our energy wisely. This is also emphasized in traditional decks which show a figure resting behind a defensive wall of nine staves. The battle may not be over, but the figure is safe for now.

Drawing the Nine of Wands recommends you conserve your energy. If drawn in response to a stressful situation, this card counsels you to pause and reconsider. Does the situation truly merit this level of your attention? A well-placed pause can prevent you from speaking in anger or acting on impulse. As with the Nine of Discs, a pause can provide time for solitude and rejuvenation. This pause also allows you to evaluate progress. What's working? What's not? Is it possible to delegate? To delete? A few steps back and some time away allow you to make the wisest decisions. This card can also indicate a delay in plans.

The Nine of Cups

In traditional decks, a satisfied man sits in front of a table arrayed with nine chalices. New Vision shows children eating and playing in back of the table, enjoying themselves free from parental restraint. Robin Wood shows a jolly fat man standing in front of the cups. Crowley names this card Happiness. All these portrayals suggest satisfaction, a magnification of the gift of the Ace of Cups. Motherpeace and Tranquil Willows pictured here portray this as the wishing card. In Motherpeace, naked women frolic around a pool. In Tranquil Willows, a woman imbues nine cups with her wishes during a moon ceremony.

The Nine of Cups counsels careful consideration of what brings us the most joy. This task is more difficult than it seems, because often what we think we want is not what we truly want. A good approach is to carefully evaluate your life right now. When you are happiest, who are you with and what are you doing? Pay attention to this. Focus on the joy you already have in order to invite more into your life. This card also counsels you to avoid being too greedy. True satisfaction comes not from without, but from within. When drawn in response to an unresolved situation, this card suggests that your wishes will be granted.

Tens

Accomplishment and Transformation

The Ten of Discs

Named Wealth, this card in Crowley's Thoth deck shows ten coins forming the pattern of the Tree of Life, suggesting riches in all areas of life. Many decks, like Tranquil Willows shown above, focus on the wealth of home and family. Motherpeace focuses on the wealth of community. Waldherr's Lover's Path and Motherpeace suggest reward at the end of effort. Lover's Path presents a golden gate opening onto a mansion cradled in green hills, signifying the end of Danae's long journey. Motherpeace illustrates a woman giving birth. Her healthy child is the culmination of gestation. Many decks reflect the serenity that wealth brings.

Drawing the Ten of Discs portends material blessings that we have worked for or inherited and emphasizes the security that comes from such riches. This card may indicate the successful culmination of a business or real estate deal. The Ten of Discs may also refer to the safety net of people who are there to catch you when you fall and to provide what you lack. When drawn with the Five of Discs or Eight of Swords, this card suggests that you need to open your eyes to the gifts in front of you. You may also need to increase your sense of *havingness,* your ability to accept the wealth available to you.

The Ten of Swords

A figure lies on the ground, stabbed through the back with ten swords. This image is shown in Tranquil Willows pictured here and in many other decks. New Vision reveals a cloaked figure viewing the body – whether he is a surprised observer or the murderer is unclear. Motherpeace depicts ten priestesses jumping off a cliff, abandoning their temple to invaders. Crowley names this card Ruin and presents ten broken swords. Waldherr's decks are more positive. Goddess Tarot reveals a fence of ten woven swords in the sky, suggesting wisdom after tribulation. Lover's Path shows an array of nine arrows accompanied by lightning. White wings bring the tenth arrow, promising enlightenment.

Drawing the Ten of Swords reflects a surrender of what you have been trying desperately to control. The nightmare inner journey of the Nine of Swords is over. Transformation has occurred. While you may be feeling the pain of loss, the overriding result is a sweet release. This card indicates acceptance of *what is* instead of *what you want it to be.* The Ten of Swords signals a surrender of hopes that will not be fulfilled, a surrender of plans that will not come to fruition. When drawn in response to a relationship question, this card indicates that it is time to let go.

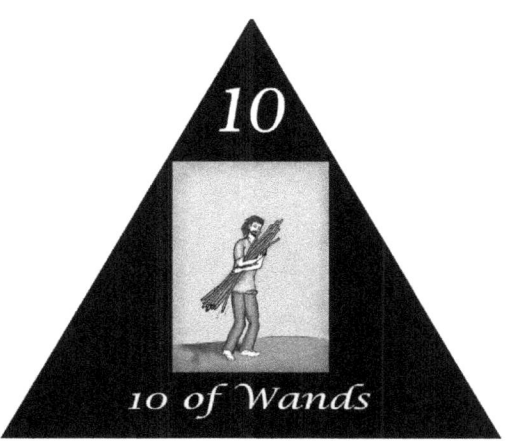

The Ten of Wands

A man struggles under the awkward and heavy bundle of wands in Tranquil Willows shown above and in most traditional decks. In Waldherr's Goddess Tarot, ten wands are woven together into a gate, depicting the completion of effort. New Vision portrays the labor involved with harvesting fields, emphasizing that successfully tended crops will result in an increased workload. Similarly, success in any business venture usually brings added work and responsibility. Crowley's Thoth names this card Oppression, suggesting that the heaviness of work can weigh us down. In contrast, Motherpeace shows an ecstatic dance and drum circle, portraying the cathartic release of pent up energy.

Drawing the Ten of Wands suggests you feel overburdened by work and have a strong desire to lay that burden down. Your struggle under increased responsibilities and commitments is a byproduct of your success. However, this card also cautions you not to make things harder than they need to be. This applies to social situations and relationships as well as to work. When drawn with the Eight of Discs or the Hanged One, you are counseled to stop micromanaging. Like the advice of the Nine of Wands, it would be helpful to carefully evaluate what you can do to lighten your load.

The Ten of Cups

Ten chalices appear with a rainbow in the sky in traditional decks. A couple, often shown with young children, greets the rainbow with joy. Motherpeace depicts Native Americans celebrating rain in the arid Southwest. A huge flowering tree appears under the rainbow of cups in Waldherr's Lover's Path. This is the tree which grew from the bodies of the star-crossed lovers Tristan and Isolte. All these portrayals reflect a renewal of hope and joy at the end of a long struggle. Tranquil Willows pictured here shows couples dancing at a formal affair, perhaps an anniversary celebration. A fountain of artfully stacked chalices forms a centerpiece.

Drawing the Ten of Cups highlights emotional satisfaction, especially in relationships. When drawn with the Five of Cups or Eight of Swords, this card suggests that you have closed yourself off from the bliss that could be yours, perhaps because you are wedded to resentment over a past hurt. Drawing the Ten of Cups with the Eight of Cups suggests that part of your life is satisfying, and part is not. You may need to let go of what no longer satisfies before you can claim the joy available to you. If drawn in the midst of a dark time, the Ten of Cups promises a joyful end to that journey.

The Court Cards

Modern playing cards have three face cards or *court cards* – the king, the queen, and the jack. But older playing card decks included as many as six face cards per suit. From the earliest extant to the most modern deck, Tarot usually includes four court cards – the king, the queen, the knight, and the page – although many modern decks, including Tranquil Willows featured here, rename and reinterpret these cards.

One of the most unusual reinterpretations of the court cards is Crowley's in his Thoth deck. In Thoth, queens are the highest face card, followed by knights. Crowley adds princes, and pages become princesses. This can cause confusion to those who come to Crowley from a more traditional deck, especially because Crowley's knights (standing in for kings) are close in meaning to the traditional knights. Thus the meanings assigned to traditional kings have been left out of this deck, and princes are given essentially new meanings.

Vicki Nobel and Karen Vogel were influenced by Crowley's court cards when they created their deck. Nobel's and Vogel's Motherpeace was perhaps the first deck to offer an entirely new vision of these cards – naming them shamans (kings), priestesses (queens), sons (knights), and daughters (pages) – although many subsequent decks rename the court cards in a similar fashion. Tranquil Willows featured here uses the signifiers wisdom (kings), adepts (queens), warriors (knights), and students (pages).

While the court card interpretations presented here owe much to Crowley's Thoth and Motherpeace, the traditional names are used for clarity.

Pages

Exuberance and Youthfulness

The Page of Discs

Many decks portray a young man or woman holding up a disc and focusing attention on it. Traditional images of Pages dovetail with traditional images of Aces – the gift that was offered by a giant hand has been accepted by a youthful person. Robin Wood shows light streaming out of the disc, emphasizing the message of a divine gift. Both Crowley's Thoth and Waldherr's Lover's Path show a woman holding a disc, but her eyes are closed and her focus is inward. Motherpeace takes this interpretation one step further, showing a woman on a vision quest. In Tranquil Willows pictured here, the student wears the solar cross on her necklace, representing earth.

Drawing the Page of Discs counsels journeying within to discover what you already know subconsciously. Just as with a vision quest, however, the answers received may be cryptic. While a general direction will be clear, you may be required to move forward without having all the answers. This is especially true when drawn with the Moon. The Page of Discs may indicate that you are beginning a new phase of personal growth and self-discovery, a phase that includes meditation or a similar practice. This card may also indicate that you are conceiving a new idea, plan, or creative project.

The Page of Swords

The Ace of Swords is put into action in many depictions of this card: a young person slices a sword through the air. A sense of recklessness pervades these images. The viewer wonders if the figure is skilled enough to handle this power. In Robin Wood, the shining sword is a guide, leading a girl as she runs forward. In Waldherr's Lover's Path, Psyche throws an arrow down to earth. In Crowley's Thoth and Motherpeace, a figure on a mountaintop wields the sword to transform ideas and words into physical forms. In Tranquil Willows pictured here, the student wears a sword on her necklace, representing air.

Drawing the Page of Swords reflects an exuberance of energy which sometimes manifests as frustration or impatience. This card often appears when we are held up by limited means or by others who are slow to act. The counsel of this card is to channel all that energy into a different direction – temporarily. This card does not suggest abandoning your plans. When drawn with the Three of Wands or the Wheel, the message is that action that will be beneficial to you later is happening out of view. When drawn with the Hanged One, you may need to wait and try a different approach later.

The Page of Wands

A young person contemplates a tall walking stick or wand, indicating a new direction, in many portrayals of this card. New Vision also reveals a background figure walking off in the opposite direction, indicating the path not taken or left behind. Motherpeace, Waldherr's Lover's Path, and Crowley's Thoth show a figure exuberantly rushing forward. The figure in Motherpeace leaps forward, accompanied by a goat and geese. The figure in Goddess Tarot charges ahead on a white horse. The figure in Thoth rises upwards, holding a tiger by the tail. In Tranquil Willows pictured here, the student wears a wand on her necklace, representing fire.

Drawing the Page of Wands indicates liberation of spirit and rushing towards freedom – moving ahead, moving on, starting a new direction. This card may appear after you have mastered a *beast* that you have been fighting for some time. This beast may represent a part of yourself that has needed to change or some person or situation that has been standing in your way. If you are not feeling free when you draw this card, ask yourself what would make you feel liberated. What needs to change inside or outside of yourself, and what can you do to bring about this change?

The Page of Cups

A fish rises out of a chalice, giving a secret message to the youth holding the cup. This is the central image in traditional decks. Waldherr's Goddess Tarot shows a young woman drinking deeply from a cup, communing with her feelings. Crowley's Thoth shows a woman mostly underwater, connecting with a sea turtle and a fish. A swan rests on her head as she reemerges, suggesting insight gained from emotions. Motherpeace shows a naked figure bathing in a pool under a waterfall. A jug rests on a turtle's back, collecting a sample of the experience. In Tranquil Willows pictured here, the student wears a cup on her necklace, representing water.

Drawing the Page of Cups indicates being overwhelmed by emotions, just as we were during the wild hormonal fluxes of puberty. Nearly anything can trigger an outburst. If this card represents someone close to you, give that person leeway and compassion. If you are the troubled one, do your best to cope. Make room in your life to feel your feelings – let them flow rather than damming them up. As the Thoth deck reminds us, insight will result. However, now is not the time to make decisions or take action. This period of difficulty will pass. Do your best to be gentle with yourself and kind to others.

Knights

Movement and Force of Will

The Knight of Discs

A knight on a horse holds a golden disc before him like a guiding light in the traditional depiction of this card. Waldherr's Lover's Path and Goddess Tarot show a prince holding a disc as he walks forward. The large gold coin represents his power and wealth. Crowley's Prince rides a chariot pulled by a bull, a globe at his side. A winged bullhead tops his helmet, signifying determination and movement. Tranquil Willows' Warrior above holds a hatchet. The silver disc is his shield. Motherpeace presents an archer whose arrow is ready to fly forward and hit the center of the target.

Drawing the Knight of Discs signals that you are right on the mark. If you have been questioning your path or your plans, this card gives you the go-ahead to proceed. While you may face some challenges along the way, you are well equipped to meet them head-on. You have won recognition for your skills from those around you, and you have the necessary determination to succeed. When this card represents someone close to you, allow him to serve as your champion. He makes an excellent advocate and ally. When this card represents someone in opposition to you, consider the possibly that he may be in the right.

The Knight of Swords

Sword held aloft, a knight charges forward with great speed, as shown in most traditional decks. He is practically airborne in his haste. Robin Wood shows the knight literally airborne on a white pegasus, wearing a winged helmet. He rides through the clouds, lightning forking from his sword. Waldherr's Lover's Path depicts Cupid in the clouds, sending his arrows where they are needed. Motherpeace portrays a Roman Centurion strangling a dove while eyeing a treasure chest, emphasizing the negative attributes a Warrior can have. Tranquil Willows above emphasizes the positive, showing a warrior practicing the discipline her craft requires. Crowley's Prince holds the reins on several small versions of himself, reins he is now ready to cut.

Drawing the Knight of Swords may indicate that you or someone close to you is impetuously rushing forward. The motivation behind this movement may be breaking out of bonds that have been holding you back. In that case, this momentum and determination is a gift that will help you achieve that end. However, if this card is drawn in response to a question about a new involvement, caution is advised, especially in regards to a new relationship.

The Knight of Wands

Traditional decks depict this knight charging forward on a horse, the red plumes on the knight's helmet and shirt suggesting flames. In Robin Wood, the knight's fiery horse sports a mane and tail of flame. The Warrior in Tranquil Willows shown above twirls a staff with flames at both ends. Crowley's Prince drives a chariot of literal fire, a lion pulling him forward through a field of flames. All this fire imagery emphasizes passion of the heart and spirit. Waldherr's decks and Motherpeace depart from this. Lover's Path and Goddess Tarot portray a young man on a journey, long walking stick at his side. Motherpeace presents a sacred clown, dancing for his people.

The Knight of Wands often appears when you are wondering whether or not to proceed, especially in a situation where you feel vulnerable. This card counsels moving forward with an open heart and being more open about who you are. Being more open can cause you to be the center of attention in a way that you're not quite comfortable with and may set in motion events that are out of your control. While this can bring discomfort and uncertainty, it will eventually bring a more authentic way of living. This card counsels going with the flow to discover where life will take you.

The Knight of Cups

The golden chalice this knight holds consumes his attention in traditional decks' portrayal of this card. Head bowed, foreleg raised, his horse prepares to step into a river. In Robin Wood, this knight rides a hippocampus, half horse, half fish. Together they journey through the sea. A heart appears on this knight's cup, and a slight smile graces his lips. Crowley's Prince flies a chariot pulled by an eagle. They skim over the water. His attention is focused on the serpent coiling up out of the cup he holds. Motherpeace shows a man miraculously floating on the sea in Sukhasana pose. The Tranquil Willows Warrior shown above paints chalices in quiet contemplation.

Drawing the Knight of Cups counsels a need for more self-awareness. Fearful of confronting what resides in their hearts, many people choose to instead numb-out via one of the many easy methods popular culture provides. This card cautions that someone – you or someone close to you – is not being honest about what she feels and what she wants. If this problem is not remedied, heartache will result. The first step is self-exploration via meditation or therapy. A regular Tarot practice is one way to become more aware. When this card applies to a relationship, both people must have self-knowledge before they can be honest with each other.

Queens

Empowerment and Inspiration

The Queen of Discs

Traditional decks show a queen sitting on her throne on a green hillside. She cradles the golden disc in her lap, much as she would a child. A rabbit in the corner of the card represents fertility. New Vision shows an image on the back of her throne: the queen giving alms to the poor. Motherpeace shows a mother meditating outdoors with a child by her side. Crowley's Thoth shows the queen wearing an enormous headdress of curled horns. A globe rests in the crook of her arm. Tranquil Willows' Adept-queen is shown above. Her earth symbol is a four-colored medicine wheel overlaid by a Celtic knot.

The Queen of Discs is about self-care. Drawing this card reminds you to take care of your body. This includes getting enough sleep, eating healthy foods, exercising regularly, and reducing your stress. If you have been lacking in these areas, this card serves as a warning to remedy that before serious problems occur. If you have been postponing starting that special diet your practitioner recommended, putting off joining a yoga studio, or failing to book your next acupuncture or massage appointment, the Queen of Discs reminds you that now is the time. When drawn with the Five of Discs, the message is doubly strong.

The Queen of Swords

Sword held high in one hand, the other hand raised in an emphatic gesture, this queen sits high on a hill in traditional decks. The viewer can almost hear her saying, "make it so." The queen's gesture in Robin Wood is different. Arm raised with palm up, she seems to be sending off a wish. This theme is further exemplified in Motherpeace, where a woman sends forth an owl from a snowy mountaintop under a full moon. The queen in Crowley's Thoth has just cut off a man's head. She reposes on a throne made of clouds. Tranquil Willows' Adept, shown above, looks resolved.

The Queen of Swords is about clarity and the power of words. Drawing this card counsels you to speak your truth with the confidence of a queen. Directness and specificity are required. When drawn with the Page of Discs or the Knight of Cups, this card advises you to look within for more clarity before you start issuing orders. It could be that you are stuck in an old role that must be jettisoned before you can step into your power. When drawn with the Magician, the Queen of Swords advises you to use your words in the service of manifesting a goal or creative project.

The Queen of Wands

Crowley portrays this queen as a giantess. Flames leap from her crown and surround her. Her right hand rests on the head of leopard. In Waldherr's Lover's Path, the Norse goddess Fricka holds a pot of flames in her lap. Robin Wood and traditional decks stylize this flame imagery in the queen's bright yellow gown and in sunflowers. The feline in these decks is a black cat, signifying good luck. This theme is emphasized in Motherpeace by a rainbow ending in a pot of gold. Tranquil Willows' Adept shown above is backed by a wand with a glowing crystal tip, signifying the power to manifest.

The Queen of Wands is about focus and fiery determination. Drawing this card counsels you to take action on your dreams and goals. The person this queen represents brings a revitalizing energy with her wherever she goes. She acts as a catalyst for those she comes in contact with, encouraging them to apply for that Master's program, book that trek across Alaska, or finally put together that portfolio to earn a gallery show. If you draw this card at a time you feel discouraged or feel in danger of abandoning your dreams, the Queen of Wands encourages you to redouble your efforts.

The Queen of Cups

The ocean plays a central role in many decks' depictions of this queen. Traditional decks show her foot resting at the water's edge. Robin Wood shows her foot in the water. Motherpeace portrays her as a mermaid singing by the water. Crowley presents this queen submersed to her knees. In all of these portrayals, the ocean represents the world of dreams. Most of these queens hold a cup. In traditional decks, she holds an elaborate ciborium, the sacred vessel that contains the consecrated host in Catholic mass. The cup in Robin Wood is covered by a cloth, rays of light radiating out. The Adept in Tranquil Willows shown above deeply inhales the mist rising from her cup.

The Queen of Cups is about inspiration. Drawing this card advises you to pay attention to what you dream about at night and to the thoughts that niggle at the edge of your consciousness. These can point to something much deeper and may provide the key you need to unlock a troubling situation in your life. Similarly, seemingly random thoughts – such as song fragments and lines from films – may be gifts from your muse, gifts you can integrate into your creative projects. Drawing this card can also encourage you to be an inspiration to others, whether directly or by example.

Kings

Wisdom and Experience

The King of Discs

In traditional decks, this king's robe is covered with grapevines, and he sits amongst fruiting vines which symbolize fertility and prosperity. Under his elaborate robe, however, he wears a suit of armor, and his foot rests on a tiger's head. Four bullheads grace his throne. In addition to his crown, he wears laurel leaves. In Waldherr's Lover's Path, this king is Zeus. Robin Wood crowns this king with grape leaves, suggesting Bacchus. In Motherpeace and Tranquil Willows pictured here, this figure is female. Motherpeace depicts her as a traveling shaman guided by an eagle. Tranquil Willows depicts her as a church elder in front of a stained glass window representing the four-colored medicine wheel.

The King of Discs is about staying grounded and trusting your experience. Drawing this card assures you that no matter what the situation, you are up to the challenge. Your decisions will naturally emerge from the depth of your character. When drawn with the Emperor, this card suggests that you will be called upon to advise or even make decisions for others who are less capable. When drawn in times of upheaval, this card counsels you to find ways to ground yourself. This includes regularly eating and sleeping, spending some time outdoors, pausing to breathe deeply, and ensuring that your territory is secure.

The King of Swords

In Robin Wood, a battle leader in a winged helmet stands in the middle of a field, arms crossed, sword held aloft. Clearly no one will be able to pass unchallenged. Traditional decks show this king seated on his throne at the edge of cliff, defending his territory. New Vision shows an infant behind the king's throne, protected by the boundary created by a sword on the ground. In Waldherr's Lover's Path, this king is Adonis, ruling from the clouds. Motherpeace and Tranquil Willows portray this figure as female. Motherpeace illustrates the power of her words leading others to a new dimension. The wise woman in Tranquil Willows shown above is backed by a sword that transmits lightning bolts.

The King of Swords is about protection and wise words. Drawing this card encourages you to take whatever steps are needed to protect yourself, starting with verbally setting boundaries. This card magnifies your voice, indicating that others are now more likely to pay attention to what you say. This card also counsels listening to the wisdom of someone you respect and carefully considering his advice. Drawing this card with Justice indicates that you are being called on to be an advocate for someone else. Drawing this card with Strength suggests that someone may need your protection.

The King of Wands

The Norse god Wotan wanders a forest in Waldherr's Lover's Path. His eye patch reminds viewers that he gave up his eye in order to obtain wisdom. Robin Wood depicts this king's charisma through his stance and dress. He stands with one foot slightly forward and one palm held up, inviting openness. He wears a flame-red and gold cape adorned with lion imagery. This lion imagery also appears in traditional decks. Robin Wood, Motherpeace, and Tranquil Willows pictured here all portray this king with a pleasant expression on his face. Motherpeace backs this figure with Egyptian gods, emphasizing his authority.

The King of Wands is about penetrating insight and skillful negotiation. Drawing this card forewarns that you may be placed in a position of brokering an agreement between warring factions, whether in a business, family, or social situation. It may also indicate you will find yourself caught in an underlying quagmire of conflicting loyalties and agendas that you were previously unaware of. The King of Wands counsels you to proceed with caution and skepticism in order to avoid being misled by surface appearances. This card calls upon you to use your charisma and authority for positive ends.

The King of Cups

Traditional decks depict this king mysteriously floating on a stone slab in the middle of the ocean. He wears a golden fish around his neck, and a fish leaps in the background, symbolizing a connection between the conscious and the unconscious. In Waldherr's Lover's Path, this king is Mark who was betrayed by his wife Isolte. He has mastered his emotions and has achieved peace. New Vision shows a giant wave approaching the king, yet the tools shown behind his throne suggest he is fully equipped to deal with any difficulties. In Motherpeace and Tranquil Willows, this figure is female. In Motherpeace, she wears a mask. In Tranquil Willows above, she wears an expression of calm confidence.

The King of Cups is about staying on an even keel and masking your emotions. Drawing this card indicates that you may be placed in a position where it is inappropriate for you to express your emotional response. This may occur when you are serving in a professional capacity or when you are caring for the young, the elderly, or the ill. This self-restraint is necessary in such situations, but can take a toll on you over time. Increased self-care is needed after hours to reduce your stress. A cathartic release may be required. Find safe ways to obtain that – perhaps through vigorous exercise or through watching a tearjerker.

Reading the Cards

Getting Started

Learning the Cards

I suggest you begin by choosing a deck that attracts you. You can view images from many different decks online to find one that resonates with you. If you are looking for a quick start, there are several good "Tarot for Beginners" books available. *Tarot in Ten Minutes* by R. T. Kaser is a fun one I would recommend. However, memorizing a few key phrases doesn't make someone a Tarot reader, just as learning a few chords doesn't make someone a musician. There is no substitute for regular practice.

I suggest that you set aside a regular time to work with the cards – daily is best, but weekly or even monthly will also suffice, as long as you are consistent. If you decide to work with the cards daily, draw one card each day during your regular meditation time. If weekly, meditate on a card or to do a multiple card reading, perhaps every Saturday morning or every Sunday afternoon. If monthly, perhaps the first of the month or the first Saturday of the month would suit – or even on the full moon. Find the time that works best for you.

Consistency is key is the overriding principle for getting to know the cards. Only by working with the cards regularly and observing how they play out in your life can you grow to understand the depth of meaning each card carries. No book of interpretations can substitute.

If you are unfamiliar with your deck, I suggest you begin by meditating on your cards for a few months before asking them questions. Before you begin the practice of shuffling the cards and choosing one or more at random, try turning the cards face up and choosing an image that attracts you. The *Tarot for*

Meditation exercises later in this book are also a good way to get to know the cards.

If you have decided to work with the cards daily, you may want to draw the cards in order. For example, the Ace of Discs, then the Two of Discs, then the Three of Discs, and so forth. Many decks tell a story through each Minor Arcana suit, and all decks tell a story through the Major Arcana. It is important to be familiar with the stories your deck tells.

I strongly recommend you dedicate a notebook as a Tarot journal. This notebook should have enough pages for you to devote two or three to each of the 78 cards, writing the names of the cards on your journal pages. Begin with the Major Arcana – The Fool, 0, through The World, XXI. Then record the Minor Arcana cards by suit, for example, the Ace through the King of Discs, the Ace through the King of Wands, and so forth.

As you read the interpretations of the cards, take notes in your journal. Don't copy down the meanings word for word. Instead, read the information in this book, then close it, and jot down in your own words what stands out most in your mind. Keep your comments brief. Leave plenty of room to add more comments later. Think of this journal as your personal reference book.

If you also keep a personal journal, you can use that to explore the cards in greater depth, specifically noting which life events you associate with the cards you draw. Doing so gives you a living, breathing knowledge of the cards that no book-learning can replace.

Reading the Cards

Once you are familiar with your deck and you feel you are ready to begin asking it questions, I suggest you begin with a small reading, one to three cards, then gradually progress to larger spreads, for example, a three-card reading, then a five-card reading, then a seven-card reading, and so forth, over a period of weeks or months. Be certain you feel you have mastered the smaller readings before you progress to larger spreads. Some sample spreads are given below. I suggest that in the beginning of your practice, you ignore reversed or tilted card meanings and just read the cards upright. There is a section on card orientation in Advanced Readings later in this book.

It may be best to begin by asking for general guidance for a specific time period – today, this week, the month – or for a specific situation – at my job, in this friendship, about this conflict.

Before you begin any reading, seclude yourself in a quiet space where you won't be interrupted and are free from electronic distractions. You may wish to create a small ritual for yourself to enter into a meditative state, such as lighting a candle or incense or just taking off your shoes and doing some deep breathing. You may have a special cloth you would like to lay the cards on. Again, consistency is key. Once you find something that works for you, do it every time.

Shuffle the cards and hold them in your hands as you focus on your question. When you feel you are ready, begin cutting the cards, and keep cutting them until you feel the right card is on top. Draw this card and place it face up on the surface in front of you. Continue this process until you have drawn all the cards for your spread.

Begin by examining the card yourself before you look up the meaning. What do the image, card title, and card number convey to you? What's going on in the card? How do the colors make you feel? And so forth. Then look up the meaning and relate it to your intuitive interpretation, making notes in your Tarot journal. If you keep a personal journal, I recommend you write down your card readings by date. Alternately, you can take a photo of the card spreads and keep a record that way.

Beginner Card Spreads

One Card: Overview

What's going on? Draw one card with the intent to see what the situation is. Ask yourself what this card reveals about you in relation to the other people in the situation. This card will become the first card in the advanced Celtic Circle spread.

Sample Reading

The Tower. As a one-card overview, The Tower shows that a big shake-up and restructuring is at hand. This may be mostly internal, such as falling into or out of love, or mostly external, such as relocating for a job.

One Card: Action

Draw one card with the intent to see what action you should take in the situation. Be aware that the answer may be "take no action now" or that the action may be internal rather than external. Use your intuition.

Sample Reading

Seven of Discs. As a one-card action reading, this says both "wait" and "have faith." All possible action has already been taken. Now it's time to turn your attention to something else while waiting to see what happens.

Three Cards: Overview - Action - Outcome

Lay out the cards side by side, left to right. The first card you draw reflects the overview of the situation you asked about. The second card reflects the action you should take. The third card reflects the outcome, if things keep going the way they are now.

Sample Reading

1-Overview: Four of Cups

2-Action: Queen of Swords

3-Outcome: The Magician

You are not happy with any of the choices being offered. The cards counsel speaking up about what you really want. The results will be positive. Now is a good time – magic is on your side!

Three Cards: Past - Present - Future

This spread gives you a view of a situation over time. Lay out the cards side by side, left to right. The first card you draw reflects what was happening in this situation in the past, perhaps pointing to a key element that you may have missed. The second card reflects the situation at the present moment, emphasizing the current challenge or blessing. The third card reflects the future for this situation, drawing your attention to what's most important.

Sample Reading

1-Past: The Lovers

2-Present: Seven of Wands

3-Future: Four of Wands

A relationship has grown into maturity, but now that the rose-colored glasses phase is over, conflict has arisen. Now is the time to work things out together. Be clear. Speak up. Listen. Set some firm boundaries but compromise where possible. This relationship has a strong future, possibly even marriage, if you are both willing to carefully work through this stage.

Five Cards: Snapshot

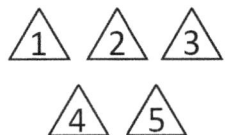

Add an Action card and an Overview card to the Past-Present-Future spread above. Place these side by side in a row under the first three cards. This spread is designed to give you a quick snapshot of a situation. An expansion of the three-card sample reading given above shows how the five-card spread provides more information.

Sample Reading

1-Past: The Lovers

2-Present: Seven of Wands

3-Future: Four of Wands

4-Overview: Ten of Wands

5-Action: Son of Cups

A relationship has grown into maturity, but the rose-colored glasses phase is over, and conflict has arisen. Now is the time to work things out together. Be clear. Speak up. Listen. Set some firm boundaries but compromise where possible. This relationship has a strong future, possibly even marriage, if you are both willing to carefully work through this stage. Note however that this negotiation is hard work. Don't make it harder than it needs to be, but also don't underestimate what's involved. Commit to it and see it through. During this process it is important for both parties to pay careful attention to how they feel as things unfold, important for both parties to avoid overriding their real needs out of embarrassment or fear. Allow time for adequate self-reflection and honest sharing.

Advanced Readings

Intermediate to Advanced Card Spreads

The Celtic Circle

Three Cards: Overview - Atmosphere - Lesson

This spread is the inner circle of the large Celtic Circle spread explained below. This three-card spread is more difficult to master than the beginner three-card spreads, but it will give deeper insight into your question. These cards are laid out in a triangle.

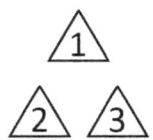

The first card you draw goes at the top of the triangle and reflects the overview of the situation you asked about. The second card is the lower left point of your triangle. It reflects the atmosphere around you right now, the thoughts and feelings relevant to your question. The third card is the lower right point of your triangle. It reflects the lesson in your life right now and could point to your challenges in the situation or how to overcome those challenges.

> ***Sample Reading***
>
> 1-Overview: The World
>
> 2-Atmosphere: Eight of Swords
>
> 3-Lesson: The Hanged One

You are in the middle of something wonderful, but you are feeling like it is terrible. You are focusing on the wrong things. You need to shift your perspective away from what you are unhappy about to what is going well. You may need to let go of something you think you want in order to get something better.

Five Cards: Add Below and Above

Start with the Overview-Atmosphere-Lesson spread above, and add two more cards.

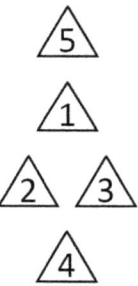

The fourth card you draw is the Below card and it is placed directly below the first three cards. The Below card is the *ground you're standing on*; it represents your subconscious, or the hidden aspects of a situation. The fifth card you draw is your Above card, and it is placed directly above the first three cards. The Above card is *in the clouds;* it represents your thoughts and projections. Both cards represent influences that are on the fringe of a situation, influences that may not fully manifest but are present.

The first five cards of the Celtic Circle — Overview, Atmosphere, Lesson, Above, and Below— are the most difficult cards to master. Keep working with them until you feel confident in interpreting these positions. Consistent practice will lead to mastery. An expansion of the three-card sample reading given above shows how the five-card spread provides more information.

Sample Reading

1-Overview: The World

2-Atmosphere: Eight of Swords

3-Lesson: The Hanged One

4-Below: Nine of Swords

5-Above: Four of Discs

You are in the middle of something wonderful, but you are feeling like it is terrible. You are focusing on the wrong things. You need to shift your perspective away from what you are unhappy about to what is going well. You may need to let go of something you think you want in order to get something better. Be aware that you are driven by fear right now, especially the fear of insecurity. Ask yourself what you need to feel safe during this time of change. Take care of yourself while still being as flexible as you can. Make sure all your physical needs are met, especially a good night's sleep. That can make all the difference in your perspective.

Seven Cards: Add Past and Future

Adding the sixth and seventh cards to the five-card core is not difficult. Card six is your *recent past.* It is placed to the left of the center three cards. Card seven is your *near future.* It is placed to the right of the center three cards. Your spread should now look like a cross with a circle within it.

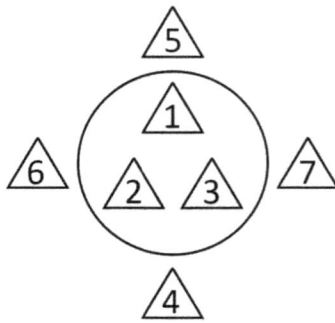

Start paying careful attention to how the cards interact with each other. Note any suits or numbers that are repeated. Note any similar messages carried by the cards. Note any cards that seem to be in opposition to each other. See how these energies, in tandem, play out in your life. An expansion of the five-card sample reading given above shows how the seven-card spread provides more information.

Sample Reading

1-Overview: The World

2-Atmosphere: Eight of Swords

3-Lesson: The Hanged One

4-Below: Nine of Swords

5-Above: Four of Discs

6-Past: Five of Wands

7-Future: The Sun

You are in the middle of something wonderful, but you are feeling like it is terrible. You are focusing on the wrong things. You need to shift your perspective away from what you are unhappy about to what is going well. You may need to let go of something you think you want in order to get something better. Be aware that you are driven by fear right now, especially the fear of insecurity. Ask yourself what you need to feel safe during this time of change. Take care of yourself while still being as flexible as you can. Make sure all your physical needs are met, especially a good night's sleep. That can make all the difference in your perspective. Recent conflicts with others in this situation have put you on edge, but your future is sunny. Focus on the small pleasures in your life and the many ways in which you are blessed.

Practice working with these seven cards for a while before you move on to the full Celtic Circle described below.

The Celtic Circle

Start with the seven-card spread above for the core of this reading. We are adding more cards to that to form the full spread. In the popular Celtic Cross spread, these cards would be added in a straight line to the right of the previous seven cards, going from bottom to top. I prefer the Celtic Circle, however, which was introduced to me (although not by that name) in *Motherpeace: A Way to the Goddess through Myth, Art, and Tarot* by Vicki Noble. In this spread, if Above is noon, the cards are added at ten o'clock, two o'clock, five o'clock, and seven o'clock respectively to complete the outer circle.

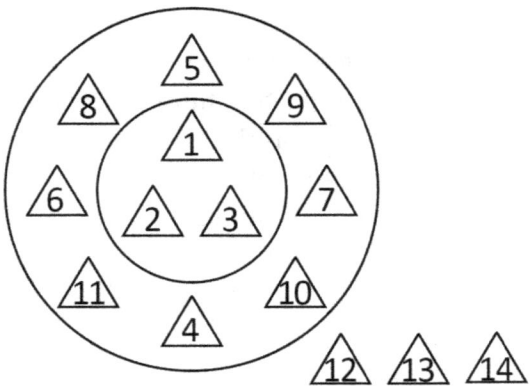

8 - Self

This card is added between Recent Past and Above at ten o'clock. This card reflects where you are at this moment in time, what your focus is, perhaps how you see yourself.

9 - House

This card is added between Above and Near Future at two o'clock. This card reveals influences around you – partners, family, friends, co-workers – and how you are currently interacting with them.

10 - Hopes & Fears

This card is added between Near Future and Below at five o'clock. Sometimes our hopes and fears are the same – we fear what we hope for the most. Use your intuition to interpret this position. If a Major Arcana card appears here, it may indicate that your hope or fear is a reality or that it has a very strong influence on the situation.

11 - Outcome

This card is added between Below and Recent Past at seven o'clock. If things keep going the way they are now, this is how they will turn out. If this is a Major Arcana card, the outcome is highly probable. If it is a Minor Arcana card, you may wish to draw one or two more cards. If no Major Arcana card is drawn, the outcome may be uncertain.

12-14 (Optional) - Action

If, after drawing the full spread, you are still uncertain about what action to take, draw one to three more cards. These cards are placed outside the circle. They give guidance on the action you should take right now, taking all factors into consideration. You may draw separate action cards for different areas of your life. For example, you may ask: What action should I take towards my partner? What action should I take at work? What financial action should I take?

When you first look at the overall spread, ask yourself: what stands out? Note suits or numbers that are repeated. Note the colors and emotional tones of the cards. Note similar messages carried by the cards. Note any cards that seem to be in opposition to each other. See how these energies, in tandem, interact.

Sample Reading

1-Overview: The World

2-Atmosphere: Eight of Swords

3-Lesson: The Hanged One

4-Below: Nine of Swords

5-Above: Four of Discs

6-Past: Five of Wands

7-Future: The Sun

8-Self: Three of Swords

9-House: The Devil

10-Hopes & Fears: Five of Swords

11-Outcome: Temperance

12-Action: Nine of Discs, Two of Swords, Empress

You are in the middle of something wonderful, but you are feeling like it is terrible. You are focusing on the wrong things. You need to shift your perspective away from what you are unhappy about to what is going well. You may need to let go of something you think you want in order to get something better.

Be aware that you are driven by fear right now, especially the fear of insecurity. Ask yourself what you need to feel safe during this time of change. Take care of yourself while still being as flexible as you can. Make sure all your physical needs are met, especially a good night's sleep. That can make all the difference in your perspective.

Recent conflicts with others in this situation have put you on edge, but your future is sunny. Focus on the small pleasures in your life and the many ways in which you are blessed.

You have recently been hurt and are afraid of being hurt more. Be aware, however, that you are projecting onto the situation. Your views are not in line with reality.

Take some extra time to yourself to heal and come to peace with the situation. A more balanced view awaits you.

Relationship Spread

This relationship spread is more useful for two people already in a relationship, but it can be used by skilled readers to predict how two potential partners could interact, especially when coupled with the numerology in the next chapter. While doing this reading, it is especially important to be clear which person is Partner 1 and which is Partner 2.

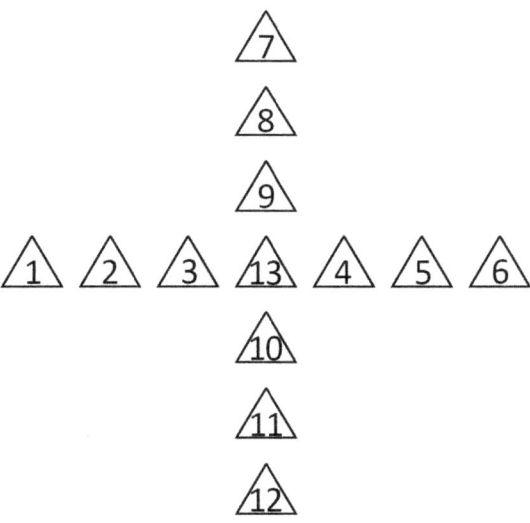

Draw three cards for Partner 1. Lay these side by side in a straight line to the left on a horizontal axis.

Draw three cards for Partner 2. Lay these side by side in a straight line to the right of the previous three cards, leaving a gap in-between the two sets of cards.

Draw three cards for the interaction of these partners together. Lay these top to bottom on a vertical axis, stopping before the row of partner cards.

Draw three cards for the action to be taken. Lay these top to bottom on a vertical axis, beginning under the row of partner cards.

Draw one card as an overview, placing it in the very middle.

Sample Reading

Partner 1 (Cards 1-3)

    The Lovers

    Queen of Wands

    Seven of Swords

    This person is still very much in love and is desperately trying to hang on to his partner, to the point of trying to manipulate the other.

Partner 2 (Cards 4-6)

    Seven of Wands

    Eight of Cups

    The Hermit

    This person is done with the relationship. She feels besieged and is ready to walk away.

Together (Cards 7-9)

    Death

    Ten of Swords

    Six of Swords

    These cards confirm that the relationship is indeed over. More work will not save it. It's time to move on.

Action (Cards 10-12)

    The Tower

    Two of Swords

    The Fool

    Allow the relationship to fall apart. Make peace with yourselves and with each other around that. It's time for new beginnings elsewhere.

Overview (Card 13)

    Ace of Swords

    Accept the truth.

Year Ahead

This spread gives a bird's eye view of what's coming up. Separate out the Major Arcana cards from your deck, shuffle them, and draw 12 cards, one for each month. Lay them out in horizontal rows of 4. Then draw one Overview card. Lay this at the top. This spread is popular at the beginning of the year (January – December), but you can start with any month.

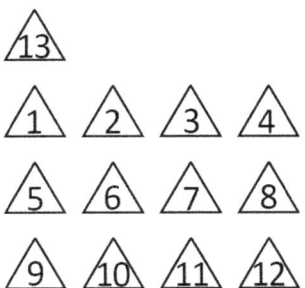

Sample Reading

13-Overview: The Hermit

This card reminds you that the answers are inside of you. The Hermit also reminds you that in order to access your inner wisdom, you must make time for solitary contemplation. The form of the contemplative work is unimportant – it could be something formal like yoga or meditation, or it could be something informal like solitary walking or journaling. Whenever in doubt, pause. Often the answers will become clear with time.

The Hermit may also indicate that you are at a crossroads of some sort. This may be an external crossroads, a beginning or ending, or it may be an internal shift in goals or perspective. Accessing your inner wisdom about this is key. Above all, trust your instincts.

1-January: The Magician

You have the mojo this month to pull off feats you wouldn't normally be able to. When the opportunity presents itself, reach a little higher, ask for a little more. The universe is on your side.

2-February: Judgement

This card indicates that some deep part of yourself has already made a decision, perhaps a crossroads decision, that you are not yet consciously aware of. The overall message here is to trust yourself, especially when you are surprised by your own words or actions. Try to move past the inner critic and go with what's happening.

3-March: The Moon

The future is unknowable from this vantage point. You

may feel you are walking forward in the dark. Focus on the ground immediately in front of you and trust that you will know what to do, step-by-step, as new terrain presents itself.

4-April: The Tower

This month brings a major shift, a restructuring, perhaps where your conscious mind catches up to your unconscious self. Don't fight it. Wait for the dust to settle; then see where you stand. Remember that the outcome will be positive, even if it is completely unexpected.

5-May: The Lovers

You feel whole again in a new way this month. This feeling could stem from a love relationship or it could stem from a new relationship with yourself, or both. Remember that love is the opposite of fear. When you find yourself in the love-fear dichotomy, choose love.

6-June: The Chariot

You feel back in the driver's seat of your life this month, centered and grounded. If you have been working on self-restraint or self-discipline in some area of your life, you experience success with that at this time.

7-July: The Hanged One

In contrast to the feeling of control last month, this month you are faced with a situation where you have no control of the outcome. The counsel here is to surrender to the best possibility for all involved, and to wait and see what happens. When in doubt, take no action.

8-August: The Empress

This is a month for nurturing yourself, for giving to yourself in the same deep way you often give to others. That may mean setting boundaries, carving out time and space for yourself. Practice the discipline of self-care.

9-September: Justice

Everything turns out just fine. If you were waiting on a resolution to a situation, you are pleased with the results. The results may be unexpected, but the solution is elegant. You may need to adjust your mindset to encompass the new reality.

10-October: The World

You see the big picture clearly and are pleased with your place in it. The perspective gives you peace. You feel well connected to your inner wisdom and to the Source this month. You see how your past connects to your present and have a clear idea of some goals for the future.

11-November: Temperance

While this card is definitely about balance, it is also about flow. In your daily life, keep an eye on how well you are balancing work and play, but also keep an eye on the flow of your thoughts, feelings, and energy. *Nothing in excess* is the advice of this card.

12-December: The Emperor

Success! You end the year on a positive note, especially in regards to work. Similar to the Magician at the beginning of the year, the Emperor has an amazing power to get things done – and to get other people to do them. Tap into that whenever possible. There may be a strong financial reward to do so.

Card Orientation

Some readers only read the cards upright, and that is a valid choice. But many readers take the orientation of the card into account. Rectangular cards can be read upright or reversed.

Reversed, or upside-down, cards can indicate several things. Sometimes a reversed card indicates that the energy of the card is suppressed or unconscious. Sometimes it indicates that the energy is overturned, already triumphed over. Sometimes it indicates there may be a negative twist on the card. The *Dark Side* sections in the *Major Arcana* chapter of this book can be read as possible reserved meanings. Use your intuition and your experience to divine the meaning of reversed cards.

Round decks, perfectly square decks, or triangular decks, such as Tranquil Willows illustrating this book, can be read with additional orientations. Cards tilted backward, or left, indicate energy held back. Cards tilted forward, or right, indicate energy outpouring, often too much energy spent. Use your intuition and your experience to divine the meaning of tilted cards.

Timeframes

Knowing the span of time that a reading covers is helpful. If reading for yourself, this largely depends on how frequently you read: if daily, the spread probably covers a short span of time, two weeks or less; if monthly, a few months; if less frequently, a longer span of time. However, you can ask the cards to reveal events over a specific period of time. For example, "show me this situation over the next three months."

Some readers use the minor arcana cards themselves to indicate time. Swords can indicate days; wands can indicate weeks; cups can indicate months, and discs can indicate years. These readers separate out the ace through ten in each suit and shuffle those to get answers about time. For example, drawing the Two of Wands would mean two weeks. Use caution, however, with this method. Try it for a few months to see how accurate it is for you before you rely on answers gained this way. The book *Tarot in Ten Minutes* by R. T. Kaser has some more complex and interesting timeframe readings that I have found to be useful.

Learning Multiple Decks

If you already know one Tarot deck well, consider learning some other decks. Working with additional decks can expand your interpretations of each card, as shown in the Sample Journal Entry below. It is important not to rush this process. Try spending a full year with a deck before moving on to another.

Choose your second, third, or fourth deck the same way you chose your first – by what attracts you. It is now possible to browse some of the images in a deck online before purchasing it. (I recommend Aeclectic.net/tarot/cards.) If there is a specific book written for the deck you choose, purchase that as well. Such books go into the deeper symbolism of those specific images, which can be helpful in expanding your interpretation of the cards.

As you learn a new deck, add to your Tarot journal, or if you are out of room, create a new one, focusing on how the cards in each deck you know expand the meaning of the card. Here's a sample journal entry for the Hierophant in different decks.

Sample Journal Entry

The Hierophant

Rider-Waite-Smith

Conventional over unconventional; inner-critic; shoulds; outer pressure to conform

Tranquil Willows

> Abuse of spiritual power; a charlatan; giving in to authority at high cost to ourselves

Crowley's Thoth

> A high priest of the Mysteries; breaking through empty ritual to find authentic spiritual connection

Waldherr's Goddess Tarot

> The positive role of tradition; the inherent power in structures such as marriage; security

Summary: When the Hierophant appears, the querent is often struggling with issues of security; is possibly facing pressure to conform or bow to authority; is wresting with making unconventional choices.

Reading for Others

Once you are mostly *off book* in reading for yourself, I encourage you to consider reading for others. Explaining the cards to others will give you a deeper knowledge of the Tarot.

I recommend you start by doing free readings for your friends who won't mind if you need to refer back to the book now and then or if your explanations are a bit awkward. Whether you only read occasionally for friends or you become a professional reader, the same principles apply.

Respect the client's confidentiality. Never reveal to anyone else the information shared in a reading. Doing so could be very damaging to your client and to your own reputation.

Be aware that people who are drawn to you for readings may be having issues similar to your own, but be careful not to project onto them. Drawing on and sharing your experience are necessary, but so is listening to the experience of the client.

People who ask you for a reading need to hear what you have to say. That's why they chose you. But they will only remember a small percentage of the reading. Don't be concerned about what they do and don't take with them at the end. They will remember what's most significant for them.

When you give a reading, give it away. Don't hang onto it. The client's pain and joy is not yours. Develop some rituals for clearing your energy and your mind after a reading. These may include a brief visualization, an affirmation, a brief stretching or deep-breathing exercise, or smudging.

Pre-reading rituals for yourself and for the client can also be helpful. This may be as simple as asking the client to hold the cards, think of her question, and take a few deep breaths while you also center yourself. A private, quiet space free from distractions is optimal for giving readings.

Feel free to decline to read for anyone at any time. If it feels wrong, don't do it. If you've already been paid, give a full refund and recommend a different reader. When in doubt, draw some cards for yourself to determine whether or not to read for that person.

The same principle applies to reading for those not present, for example, when a client asks you for information about a loved one. Ask the cards if it is right for you to look into that person; ask the cards if the client has a right to know. Use your best judgement.

Give the client the option to share as much or as little information with you as he chooses. Allow him to simply ask for a general reading. As the reading progresses, he may or may not open up more.

Be aware, in readings for yourself and others, that the cards often answer unspoken questions or speak to a deeper issue than the one named. The cards can also pick up on moods and fears. As you become more skilled, you will be able to intuit when this is happening.

I recommend you end a reading by asking if the client has a few follow-up questions, and if so, draw some cards to help answer those. I also recommend you encourage the client to jot down a few notes and to take a photo of the spread for future reference.

Numerology and Tarot

Numerology and Tarot

Numerology is based on the idea that our birthdates and our birth names can give important information about our personalities and soul paths, just as our birth times and birthplaces do in astrology. Underlying this idea is a belief that before we were born, we chose our spiritual path for this lifetime. Whether this is something you personally believe or not, many people find numerology to be strangely accurate. I rely on the Lifetime Symbol and Year Symbol in my divination work for others and consult the Name Symbol at times for additional information. I have found these symbols to be accurate in my own life as well. The system of numerology I use incorporates Tarot cards and is based on a nine-year cycle.

Lifetime Symbol

The Lifetime Symbol reflects a person's soul path in this lifetime. This is calculated by adding up the birthdate in a long line of single digits and reducing the final number to a single digit, 1 - 9. For example, if the person was born December 15, 1940, that would convert to the numbers 12, 15, 1940 (the order is not important). Add these up as single digits:

> December 15, 1940
>
> 12, 15, 1940
>
> 1+2+1+5+1+9+4+0 = 23
>
> 2+3 = 5

Be sure to include the full year, not just the last two digits. The sum of the single digits is 23. When added together (2+3), the sum is 5. The fifth Major Arcana card in the Tarot deck is the Hierophant — thus the Hierophant is the Lifetime symbol for the person whose birthdate is December 15, 1940. See the card in the *Major Arcana* section for Lifetime Symbol interpretations.

Year Symbol

The Year Symbol reflects *the location* of a person on the soul path, which we view in nine-year cycles. The Year Symbol reflects the gifts and challenges of a personal year, from one birthday to the next. This is calculated by adding the birth month and day with the year of the person's last birthday in a long line of single digits and reducing the final number to a single digit, 1 - 9. For example, if the person was born December 15, and celebrated her last birthday in 2014, that would convert to the numbers 12, 15, 2014 (the order is not important). Add these up as single digits:

December 15, 2014

12, 15, 2014

$1+2+1+5+2+0+1+4 = 16$

$1+6 = 7$

Be sure to include the full year, not just the last two digits. The sum of the single digits is 16. When added together (1+6), the sum is 7. The seventh Major Arcana card in the Tarot deck is the Chariot. Thus the Chariot is the Year Symbol for the person whose last birthday was December 15, 2014. See the card in the *Major Arcana* section for Year Symbol interpretations.

Name Symbol

A person's name at birth (including exact spellings) is needed in order to calculate someone's Name Symbol. Since this information is less available than birthdates, I use this symbol less frequently and only at the request of the client. The Name Symbol reflects the personality or *soul urge*, what people yearn for as they walk their life paths.

Using the chart below, assign a number to each letter of a person's full birth name. Add these numbers together and reduce them to a single digit.

1	2	3	4	5	6	7	8	9
A	B	C	D	E	F	G	H	I
J	K	L	M	N	O	P	Q	R
S	T	U	V	W	X	Y	Z	

Jane Michelle Smith

Jane

1+1+5+5=12 (1+2) = 3

Michelle

4+9+3+8+5+3+3+5 = 40 (4+0) = 4

Smith

1+4+9+2+8 = 24 (2+4) = 6

3+4+6 = 13 (1+3) = 4

In the example above, the name Jane Michelle Smith adds up to 13 or the single digit 4. The fourth Major Arcana card in the Tarot deck is the Emperor – thus the Emperor is this person's Name Symbol. See the card in the *Major Arcana* section for Name Symbol interpretations.

For a more in-depth look into personal numerology, I recommend Dan Millman's *The Life You Were Born to Live*.

The Interplay of Symbols

To become familiar with this style of numerology, I suggest you begin by calculating your own Lifetime and Name symbols and seeing if those ring true for you. Continue the exercise by calculating those symbols for people close to you.

If you find those interpretations resonate, calculate your current Year symbol, then calculate nine years back to the last time you experienced this Year symbol, and again to the time before that. For example, if 2014 is my Lovers year, then I last experienced a Lovers year in 2005, and I experienced a Lovers year before that in 1996. If you see a pattern in those years, calculate and reflect on other Year symbols in your past in the same way. Then do the same for people close to you.

Next consider a person's Name and Lifetime symbol together, starting with your own. How do those two symbols comment on each other? See the cards in the *Major Arcana* section for general symbol interpretations, and then use your intuition to gauge the interaction of those symbols. **Here are some examples:**

A Person's Lifetime and Name Symbols Together

In the case when a person's Lifetime and Name symbol are the same, the energy of that symbol is doubly strong. This is true for the positive as well as the negative aspects of that symbol.

Hierophant and Emperor together

This person's public persona may be charismatic. Others are naturally drawn to him for leadership and counsel. However, he may be emotionally shutdown, plagued by guilt and fear. He will experience problems in his personal life before he does the work to overcome these issues.

Justice and Hermit together

While naturally a loner, this person easily steps into an advocate role when there's a wrong to be righted. She can campaign tenaciously on behalf of others, yet may suffer from low-self esteem. She is easily drained and needs plenty of time and space to herself to stay sane.

High Priestess and Lovers together

This person easily picks up on the nuances of body language and unspoken thoughts and uses this to her advantage in her love life. She can cause trouble at times when she picks up on subtle attractions that others have no intention of revealing. Friends often seek her out for relationship advice.

Next consider how a person's Year symbol interacts with Lifetime and/or Name symbols. **Here are some examples:**

A Person's Year and Lifetime Symbols Together

Whenever you see a symbol doubled or tripled, such as a Magician Lifetime or Name symbol in a Magician year, the energy of that symbol is magnified. This is true for the gifts as well as the lessons of that symbol.

A Magician Lifetime Symbol in a Lovers Year

If this person is single and has been looking for a relationship, chances are he will find it this year. If he is already in a relationship, problems can be solved and passion rekindled this year. If this person has been feeling conflicted or pulled in different directions, an opportunity for resolution and unity will present itself this year.

An Empress Lifetime Symbol in a Lovers Year

Giving with an open hand while also setting boundaries is the focus this year, especially as that applies to love relationships. This person should be careful not to give more than she's willing to receive. She may need to step up and ask for her needs to be met. Above all, she should avoid giving with invisible strings attached.

A Chariot Lifetime Symbol in a Lovers Year

The probability of a vacation-romance is strong this year, either meeting someone new or spicing up a current relationship. Travel and love go well together at this time. This may also be a year that a friendship or relationship that's been stuck moves ahead. This won't happen on its own, however. Goals must be set and met.

Once you have a sense of how this numerology plays out in the lives of individuals, you can calculate how the symbols of different people interact. **Here are some examples:**

Interactions of People's Symbols

Whenever you see a symbol doubled or tripled, such as two people who share the same symbol, the energy of that symbol is magnified.

<u>*Person 1 (Boss) with Person 2 (Employee)*</u>

Person 1 Boss:

Lifetime Symbol Emperor & Year Symbol Empress

Person 2 Employee:

Lifetime Symbol Justice & Year Symbol Magician

This is an excellent time for the employee to ask for a raise or any other perks she feels she deserves. The Justice symbol reflects that the employee is skilled at making a case for why she deserves something more, and the Magician symbol reflects that she is likely to receive what she asks for. The boss, whose Emperor symbol reflects that he may be a bit overbearing, is now in an Empress year, a time he is more willing to be generous.

Person 1 and Person 2 (Potential Mates)

Person 1 Querent:

Lifetime Symbol Magician & Year Symbol Chariot

Person 2 Love Interest of Querent:

Lifetime Symbol High Priestess & Year Symbol Hermit

The Magician and High Priestess symbols reflect that there is strong chemistry and common interest between these two potential mates, but the year symbols indicate that now is not the best time. The love interest (with her High Priestess intuition) is fully aware of the querent's attraction to her, but the love interest is in a Hermit year and is focused on her own needs. Dating that begins now will most likely be short-term. Next year would be a better if a longer-term relationship is desired.

Try calculating the interaction of symbols for those closest to you. Whether you are reading for others or for your own enjoyment, numerology adds a deeper dimension to the Tarot.

Tarot for Meditation and Spiritual Intent

Tarot for Meditation and Spiritual Intent

Meditation with Cards

Whether you are very familiar with your cards or not familiar with them at all, meditation can help you connect more deeply with the wisdom of the Tarot. Choose a card you want to explore further or spread out your cards face up and choose a card that attracts you. Study the image carefully, paying attention to the colors, the expression on faces, the small details, and any action portrayed. The *Major Arcana* chapter above suggests you try these exercises with some specific cards for some specific purposes. These suggestions can be found in the sections titled *In Spiritual Work*.

Asking Questions

These questions can be verbalized, written, or just silently imagined. It might be helpful to take some notes at the end of the meditation in your Tarot or personal journal.

Start by asking yourself some questions:

> What general feelings does the card provoke in me?
>
> What people, situations, and events does the card remind me of?
>
> What do I think just happened in this card?
>
> What do I think will happen next?
>
> How do I feel about the place shown in this card?
>
> How do I feel about the people shown in this card?
>
> What does this card tell me about my specific situation?

You can extend this line of questioning by asking why? How so? How do I know?

Then ask some questions of the characters or even items in the card, based on what you discovered above. Some examples are:

>Who are you?
>
>What just happened?
>
>What is about to happen?
>
>What do you want to happen?
>
>What powers do you have?
>
>What motivates you?
>
>How can you help me?

Add any questions that pertain to your specific purpose. Some examples are:

>What can you tell me about _____?
>
>What do you suggest I do about _____?

Projecting Yourself into the Card

This exercise can be done with eyes opened or closed. After carefully studying the card, imagine yourself in that landscape. Allow your projected-self free reign to wander into areas not shown on the card and to interact with people in the card. Instead of asking questions, as you did in the exercise above, attempt to *be part of* the card. Allow your intuition and impulses to lead where you go and what you do and say. Relax into it.

Be sure you have a quick and easy method of ending the visualization if you start to feel uncomfortable. For example, saying "home, home, home" is one easy way to bring yourself back into the present. Take some notes at the end of the meditation in your Tarot or personal journal.

Inviting a Tarot Character into Your Dreams or Meditations

You may also invite a card character into your dreams or meditations by visualizing them there before you go to sleep or before you begin your meditative session. Similar to the projection exercise above, you will not know in advance what will happen. Simply be open to the experience and the messages you receive. Take some notes on the experience in your Tarot or personal journal after you wake up or after the meditation ends.

It is important that you have studied the card carefully before you do this and that you feel safe with the character. If you have a home altar or spiritual space, I suggest you lay out the card you are working with face up so that you can see it throughout the day as you walk by, better anchoring the card in your subconscious.

Cards as Focal Point in Prayer or Ritual

No matter what your spiritual practice, Tarot cards can be incorporated (unless your religion specifically forbids them). The best way to begin is to carefully consider your current practice and evaluate how the images from the cards can enhance that. If you don't want to use an actual card, you can always use a photocopy. (Most home-office printers will produce high-quality images.) If you are not religious, you may still find that creating a dedicated space for the cards, on a dresser top or small table, enhances your Tarot practice.

Laying Cards on Your Altar

The easiest way to incorporate the cards into prayer or ritual is to lay a card face up in your spiritual space so that you can see it during prayer, meditation, or ceremony. As you become adept at choosing cards, you can expand this practice by laying out several cards at once.

This card layout can be as simple as selecting a few from your daily or weekly reading to fan out where you can see them, or as complex as creating a Tarot spell with multiple layers. One technique that anyone can use is to lay out the same card from all your decks. For example, you can lay out several Magicians in a straight row to invite more magic into your life. You can lay out cards to represent specific people or qualities. For example, your Lifetime Symbol crossed by the Four of Discs is a simple protection spell.

In Spiritual Work in the *Major Arcana* chapter above suggests some specific cards to use for specific purposes. The main requirement for this kind of spiritual work is a clear intent. As you lay out the cards, be clear about what you are trying to attract. Leave the cards up for several days. Remind yourself of the intention whenever you look at them. While this work can be completely intuitive, I recommend Janina Renée's *Tarot Spells* for those who are looking for more guidance.

Using Cards with Prayer Candles

Candles, oils, crystals, religious statues, and other symbolic items can also be laid out with Tarot cards as part of your spiritual practice. A word of caution: if you burn candles and drip oil or holy water near your cards, your cards may be slightly damaged. Many people see this as a way of *blessing* their cards. Others prefer their decks to remain unmarked.

A safe and easy way to combine a Tarot card with a prayer candle is to color-photocopy a Tarot card and glue-stick the image onto a seven-day, plain glass jar candle. (In many areas of the country, these jar candles can be found in the Hispanic foods section of grocery stores or in *supermercados*.) Ideally, you will light the candle and let it burn for several days until it burns out. However, if you burn the candle unsupervised, be sure it is in a fire-safe location, like a stovetop or fireplace. If you need to blow out the candle when you leave the house, relight it when you return, and let it burn for as long as you can. Repeat as often as necessary.

As with laying out cards, the main requirement for successful candle work is a clear intent. Focus your mind on what you are trying to attract as you light the candle. As the candle burns, remind yourself of the intention whenever you look at it. For those looking for more instruction in this kind of work, I recommend Gamache's classic *Master Book of Candle Burning*. This book incorporates Psalms, which may appeal to those of a Judeo-Christian background, but does not include Tarot cards.

Index of Topics for Suggested Spiritual Work

See the *Major Arcana* chapter above for suggested spiritual work on the following topics:

    Balance (see *In Spiritual Work* for Temperance)

    Change (see *In Spiritual Work* for the Wheel)

    Creativity (see *In Spiritual Work* for the Empress)

    Decisions (see *In Spiritual Work* for the Hermit)

    Entrapment (see *In Spiritual Work* for the Devil)

    Fairness (see *In Spiritual Work* for Justice)

    Good Judgement (see *In Spiritual Work* for Judgement)

Happiness (see *In Spiritual Work* for the Sun)

Hope (see *In Spiritual Work* for the Star)

Letting Go (see *In Spiritual Work* for Death)

Love (see *In Spiritual Work* for the Lovers)

Manifesting (see *In Spiritual Work* for the Magician)

New Beginnings (see *In Spiritual Work* for the Fool)

New Perspective (see *In Spiritual Work* for the Hanged One)

Power (see *In Spiritual Work* for Strength)

Restructuring (see *In Spiritual Work* for the Tower)

Security (see *In Spiritual Work* for the Hierophant)

Self-Discipline (see *In Spiritual Work* for the Chariot)

Success (see *In Spiritual Work* for the Emperor)

Truth/Illusion (see *In Spiritual Work* for the Moon)

Understanding (see *In Spiritual Work* for the High Priestess)

Victory (see *In Spiritual Work* for the World)

About the Author

Luna Blanca has been a professional Tarot reader and spiritual teacher since the late 1990s and has been working with the Tarot for over twenty years. The decks described in this book are some of her favorites. She also works with the Marseille deck and Robert Michael Place's two decks, the Angel's Tarot and Tarot of the Saints. An eclectic Pagan by faith, Luna Blanca is the author of the yearlong course White Moon Studies and the founder of the Goddess-oriented White Moon Tradition. She works under another name as a college professor, poet, and photographer. She can be reached via her website ByTheLightOf.com.

About the Artists

Rowen Saille

Rowen Saille is a psychologist with a love of symbolism and art. While more at home with thoughts and words than with easel and brush, Rowen always found that the creative process helped her understand meanings and symbolism prevalent in the cultures around the world. Art provided introspection and helped her explore the esoteric meanings traditionally ascribed to Tarot. With Tranquillity Fearn, she was able to bring her sketches to life in vibrant imagery and color. Her favorite decks include Robin Wood and Tranquil Willows. Rowen is a Rune scholar with 33 years of experience. She uses both Tarot imagery and Runes to teach introspection and self-discovery.

Tranquillity Fearn

Tranquillity Fearn's love for art started when she was a child. She has been drawing and creating since she was old enough to use a pencil and paper. She developed the technique to digitally paint the beautiful images created by Rowen Saille in the Tranquil Willows deck and helped with coloring half of the deck. Tranquillity's favorite Tarot card is the Star. Her favorite Tarot decks are Spiral Tarot, Gaian Tarot, and of course Tranquil Willows. Her faith is multi-denominational Goddess Spirituality. She is co-author of the book *The Spirituality, Magick and Ritual of the Goddess*.

Works Cited

Cavendish, Richard. *The Tarot*. Hong Kong: Chancellor, 1988.

Gamache, Henri. *The Master Book of Candle Burning: How to Burn Candles for Every Purpose*. 1940. New York: Original Publications, 1998.

Jung, Carl G. *The Archetypes of the Collective Unconscious.* Trans. Richard F. C. Hull. Vol. 9:1. 2nd ed. Princeton: Princeton U P, 1981.

Kaser, R.T. *Tarot in Ten Minutes*. New York: Avon, 1992.

Millman, Dan. *The Life You Were Born to Live: A Guide to Finding Your Life Purpose*. Tiburon, CA: HJ Kramer, 1993.

Noble, Vicki. *Motherpeace: A Way to the Goddess through Myth, Art, and Tarot*. San Francisco: Harper, 1983.

Renée, Janina. *Tarot Spells*. Woodbury, MN: Llewellyn, 2000.

Visions: Notes of the Seminar given in 1930-1934 by C. G. Jung. Ed. Claire Douglas. Vol. 2. Princeton: Princeton U P, 1997.

Suggested Reading

Arrien, Angeles. *The Tarot Handbook: Practical Applications of Ancient Visual Symbols.* New York: Penguin Putnam, 1997.

Cameron, Julia. *The Artist's Way: A Spiritual Path to Higher Creativity.* New York: Penguin Putnam, 1992.

Cavendish, Richard. *The Tarot.* Hong Kong: Chancellor, 1988.

Crawford, Saffi and Geraldine Sullivan. *The Power of Birthdays, Stars, & Numbers: The Complete Personology Reference Guide.* New York: Ballantine Books, 1998.

Gamache, Henri. *The Master Book of Candle Burning: How to Burn Candles for Every Purpose.* 1940. New York: Original Publications, 1998.

Gray, Eden. *A Complete Guide to the Tarot.* New York: Bantam, 1972.

Holloway, Gillian. *The Complete Dream Book.* Naperville, IL: Sourcebooks, 2006.

Kaser, R.T. *Tarot in Ten Minutes.* New York: Avon, 1992.

Millman, Dan. *The Life You Were Born to Live: A Guide to Finding Your Life Purpose.* Tiburon, CA: HJ Kramer, 1993.

Noble, Vicki. *Motherpeace: A Way to the Goddess through Myth, Art, and Tarot.* San Francisco: Harper, 1983.

Pascal, Eugene. *Jung to Live by.* New York: Time Warner, 1992.

Pollack, Rachel. *Seventy-eight Degrees of Wisdom: A Book of the Tarot.* San Francisco: Harper, 1997.

Renée, Janina. *Tarot Spells.* Woodbury, MN: Llewellyn, 2000.

Ziegler, Gerd. *Tarot Mirror of the Soul: Handbook for the Aleister Crowley Tarot.* San Francisco: Weiser, 1988.

www.ingramcontent.com/pod-product-compliance
Lightning Source LLC
Chambersburg PA
CBHW071157160426
43196CB00011B/2112